At the Jail on Easter Island

RADU POLIZU

AT THE JAIL ON EASTER ISLAND

COVER & BOOK DESIGN by Alexandru Oprescu

LIBRARY OF CONGRESS CATALOGING-IN-PUBLICATION DATA

At the Jail on Easter Island
Authored by Radu Polizu

ISBN: 9798994859414
LCCN: 2026938696

Acknowledgement

I want to thank the publishing house New Meridian Arts, and especially Nava Renek, whose careful, discerning eye guided the text with precision, clarity, and insight, shaping it into a coherent and compelling narrative, bringing it patiently from draft to publication.

I am also deeply grateful to Olivia Carrescia-Dinardo for her meticulous editing, for the long and thoughtful conversations that helped me clarify what I was truly trying to say, and for her patient, invaluable work in ensuring that every sentence reads smoothly and accurately.

CONTENTS

CHAPTER 1

History and Myth in the Pacific

IN MY MANY TRAVELS, I HAVE NOTICED SOMETHING striking when speaking with indigenous people. When they tell their stories, the past is never past—it is always spoken in the present. Often, they retell events that happened centuries ago with an immediacy and vividness that makes you feel as though you're witnessing breaking news. I remember a casual exchange I had with a Hopi man in Arizona. As we talked, he took a stick and began drawing a map in the dirt, narrating how the Navajo surrounded the Hopi and attacked their tribes. The urgency in his tone, the precision of the map—every detail made it seem like the events unfolded last month. Bewildered, I couldn't help but ask, "When did this happen?" He casually replied, "Oh, that was over a century ago." Even after the timeline was clarified, his story stubbornly remained in the present tense. It was clear that, for him, the events weren't just history—they were alive, still breathing within the fabric of his identity and his land.

I felt the same thing while visiting the islands in the Pacific, from the deserts of Australia to the Māori-populated corners of the Polynesian Triangle. The Pacific is a region that gives you the feeling that history and myth are not distinct entities but threads woven into a seamless tapestry of identity. Stories of creation, tribal conflicts, and ancient heroes are told with a timelessness that binds generations together. This perspective challenges our Western way of thinking, where history is boxed into books, marked by dates, and firmly separated from the present. It was this blending of history and myth that inspired me to tell the stories I discovered while walking these lands; stories of the past that continue to shape what it is now and what will be.

From the vast red deserts of Australia to the verdant valleys of Hawaiʻi, the mystical fjords of New Zealand, and the enigmatic statues of Easter Island, every corner of the Pacific whispers legends that are as alive as the landscapes they inhabit.

In Australia, the Songlines of the Aboriginal people form a spiritual map of the land, guiding travelers through the vast and harsh Outback. These Songlines, passed down through generations by oral tradition, intertwine geography and mythology, telling tales of creation and of the ancestral beings who shaped the world. The Walkabout, a rite of passage for many Aboriginal males, is more than just a journey; it is a way of connecting with these ancient stories and the land itself. Uluru, especially, is a living monument where history and spirituality converge under the endless Outback skies.

In Tasmania, the East Coast offers a journey through both natural beauty and cultural history. The beaches and forests here are not just idyllic—they are steeped in stories of the Palawa people, the island's Aboriginal inhabitants, who have lived in harmony with the land for tens of thousands of years. In the rugged west, climbing Cradle Mountain feels like ascending into a realm of myths. The alpine landscape, often shrouded in mist, evokes the ancient spirit of the land, a connection that has endured through time and tumult.

Travel further into the Pacific, and the Hawaiian Islands unfold like pages from an epic tale. Kaua'i, the 'Garden Island,' teems with legends of the Menehune—the mythical little people said to have built fishponds and temples. Oahu pulses with the energy of modernity, but beneath its bustling surface lies a deep connection to Hawaii's past, from King Kamehameha's unification of the islands to the ancient heiau (temples) scattered across the island. On Maui, while hiking through lush valleys and volcanic landscapes, you trespass into the realm of Pele, the goddess of fire and volcanoes. Pele's fiery personality, said to reside in Kilauea on the Big Island, continues to shape the land, her myth as alive as the lava that flows from the earth.

New Zealand, too, is a land where myth breathes in step with reality. The Māori people, with their rich oral traditions and intricate carvings, tell stories of legendary ancestors and gods who shaped the land. The haka, a powerful war dance, is not just a performance but an expression of identity, history, and spiritual connection. New Zealand's landscapes, immortalized in the Lord of the Rings films, echo these myths, with towering peaks and shimmering lakes that seem otherworldly. It's as if the legends of Middle-earth have merged with the Māori tales of Tūmatauenga, the god of war, and Tāne, the god of forests, creating a landscape where fiction and tradition coexist.

And then there is Easter Island, or Rapa Nui, a remote speck of land in the vast Pacific, where the *moai* statues stand as silent sentinels of a lost civilization. These colossal heads, carved from volcanic rock, are not mere sculptures—they are imbued with *mana,* the spiritual essence believed to protect the people. The Birdman cult, which emerged in the island's later history, tells of a ritual competition to select a spiritual leader, blending history, myth, and survival in a harsh and isolated environment.

The cultures of the Pacific are living proof that myth and history are not separate realms but are instead deeply intertwined. These stories are written not just in books or passed down through oral tradition—they are carved into the stone heads of Easter Island, etched into the fiery trails of Hawaii's volcanoes, and could be heard sung into the winds of Australia's Outback. Journeying through the Pacific felt like stepping into a world where legends walked beside me, guiding my path and inviting me to listen to the whispers of the land and its people.

CHAPTER 2

THE SONGLINES ARE THE RED DIRT GPS

"SLOW AND SEDENTARY PEOPLE, LIKE ANCIENT EGYPTIANS—with their concept of the afterlife journey through fields of reeds—project into the next life the journey they did not take in this life," wrote Bruce Chatwin in his book Songlines. Reading his book was my first exposure to the magical world of the Australian outback, a mysterious realm of songs and Walkabout that map its expanded spaces and the soul of its people. A world in which people decide at some point, apparently on a whim, to set off, seemingly without reason, on what may seem, for our untrained eyes, a goalless wandering. While roaming their land, they continuously hum a song that describes in detail places on their route and locations that define the space in which they live and to which they are intimately connected. For them, these are the Songlines that, if known in their entirety, would allow you to travel throughout Australia across the endless desert from ocean to ocean, without compasses or any man-made device to mark their place on the globe.

Yet Australia was not part of our travel plans. It was far, way too far. But somehow, business circumstances forced Australia to creep up on us almost unexpectedly. We crammed sleeping bags next to business suits, a backpack beside a suitcase, and boarded a plane on last-minute tickets paid for with miles. The plane was surprisingly empty, giving us several rows to stretch out during the 15-hour journey across the Pacific—an entire flight suspended over the endless blue of the ocean. In Sydney, we, along with the other passengers, were greeted by a dog that circled us several times and sniffed us intensely until it finally wagged its tail contentedly and allowed us to enter the continent. After another three hours or so in the airport, we exchanged the azure of the ocean for the red of the desert, a desert marked by shapes and lines that give the impression of dried-up rivers that have been flowing in all directions since the creation of the world. You try to find other shapes that may signal the presence of people, and very rarely, if you're lucky, you can make out a dirt road. Otherwise, there's nothing but red dirt. After four more hours, added to the thirty-eight we had already spent since leaving New York, we landed in Alice Springs, the largest town in the middle of Australia, a place seemingly conjured into existence because even the vastest emptiness needs a point of reference.

The British arrived in Australia only a couple of centuries ago, but the Outback—Australia's vast central desert—has been home to Aboriginal people for some 65,000 years. They represented an impressive diversity of ethnicities and languages, far exceeding that of Europe. The ancestors of the Aborigines migrated from Africa around 70,000 years ago, passing through Asia and Southeast Asia—then connected by low seas—before arriving in Australia. There are almost 300 languages spoken among the more than 500 tribes or 'nations' that inhabit the continent's vast expanse, with a population today of a bit under half a million people.

Aborigines did not build large stone monuments, did not form cities, did not raise animals, and did not cultivate the soil for crops. But they adapted incredibly well to the harshness of Australia's interior desert. They dug small wells, marked their locations in song, and harvested roots from sparse trees to craft the tools they needed to survive. They never developed a formal written language, yet their culture endures in rock art, extended songs, and dances accompanied by stories that could unfold over days. Some of the oldest paintings depict tall figures in traditional dress, occasionally appearing otherworldly—reminiscent, in this way, of certain depictions found in the canyons of North America. The Aborigines were able to preserve this artistic tradition. The paintings and etchings they create today closely resemble the traditional ones that were brushed onto the cave walls thousands of years ago, while the ceremonial costumes and body decorations carved in stone centuries ago are still worn in the same form in modern ceremonies.

The Aborigines live in Dreamtime. For the descendants of English settlers, at least, this Dreamtime is considered the cause that isolates them from Western society and denies them its advantages. But are there advantages of a modern society for someone who leads a life with different values? In Aboriginal belief, the Dreamtime—*Tjukurrpa* in one of their languages—marks the sacred era when ancestral beings rose from the earth and waters to roam and shape the world. The land already existed, yet was empty of content. During the initiatory journey, these ancestral beings created and named in song everything they encountered: birds and animals, hills and valleys, oceans and rivers, waterholes, rocks, mountains, and more. These Aboriginal ancestors were poets in the deepest sense of the word '*poesis*,' which means creation. When their time of caroling ended, they did not ascend to the heavens; instead, they transformed into hills or rocks, miraculous footprints on the Earth, animals or birds, freshwater holes or rivers—all vital as their songs echoed across the desert. And this Dreamtime of the Aborigines is still developing. The ancestors who came before the present-day sixth generation are considered by the Aborigines to be reborn as plants or kangaroos, becoming part of the Dreamtime. Since carbon-dating methods used by British scientists date back no further than 40,000 years, the Aborigines framed their Dreamtime around that time. The concept of Dreamtime intertwines the world's creation, the deeds of ancestral beings, the understanding of life and death, and the enduring spiritual power embedded in daily life, all unified into a singular, intricate narrative that transcends linear time. These four dimensions coexist, granting the Dreamtime supremacy over conventional notions of time and space. For Aboriginal peoples, Dreamtime represents an infinite beginning—a timeless realm where the past, present, and future converge and manifest simultaneously.

The Aboriginal religion, like other religions, is characterized by having gods who created people and the surrounding environment during a particular period at the beginning of time. All these Aboriginal deities hold multiple, sometimes overlapping roles. The Creation Beings, also known as Creation Figures, are the deities responsible for bringing people, the landscape, and all natural elements into being. Unlike gods in other religions, they were not worshipped but revered for their role in creation. Following them are the Ancestral Beings—also known as Dreamtime Ancestors—considered the direct forebears of the people living today. Their role was to teach humanity how to make tools and weapons, how to hunt animals, and obtain food. They were also responsible for the laws governing society and all ceremonies. The Aborigines believe that after death, the spirit or soul is reborn into another form of existence within the same world. Rather than taking human form, these Ancestral Beings appear as plants, animals, or outcrops of the land, each carrying the memory of deeds performed in their previous human lives.. It may be a river formed when the Rainbow Serpent crossed through that area, or an impression in a rock that might be considered the footprint or the sitting place of an Ancestral Being. Aboriginal people do not believe in animism. A rock may not possess a soul, but it might have been formed by a deity during creation. Across the continental tribes, these deities may be completely different, even for identical beliefs.

The final category comprises the Totemic Beings. They represent the original form of an animal, plant, or any other object exactly as it was conceived during the Creation Period. The Aboriginal tradition claims that each person is sourced from a specific Totemic Being. The creative spirits of the ancestors embedded elements in the landscape that were transmitted to their descendants through a symbol: a kangaroo, honey ants, a snake, a set of rocks, a spring, and many more. The totem identified their clan, shaping their extended family and, through a network of kinship ties, linking them to multiple Dreams. Aborigines originally depicted these totems and sacred places on the ground and on rocks. In modern times, the drawings have been recreated on canvas, resembling vibrant, colored visions of these sacred symbols, as though glimpsed from above. But behind the dots that seem to move on the canvas, beneath the bright colors and the elegant motives, hidden from the layman's eye is a sacred iconography.

The Aborigines name all the beings belonging to these three categories, Ancestral Beings. Any daily activity brings to the Aboriginals' minds the Ancestral Being associated with that place. If they hunt, make tools, collect bush food, or see anything in the desert, they remember the myths and the legends related to that particular Ancient Being.

To the Aborigines, their ancestors are not omnipotent gods of the material world, but demiurges who called the world into existence through song and lingered on earth, woven into the landscape as custodians of their creation. Since the spirits that named the places became part of the landscape, Dreamtime for the Aboriginal people is not merely a historical past, but an ongoing, living process. For them, time flow does not exist, so they do not say that there was a specific Dreamtime when all places were Dreamed. This Dreamtime is happening right now. This grants the Aborigines a profound connection with the land and all that inhabits it—a sacred bond, standing in stark contrast to the newly established Western society and its more self-centered values.

Aboriginal people interpret these Dreams as memories from the Creation Period, believing that in the Dream, they return to the time of the ancestors. In Aboriginal mythology, Dreamtime is not about a person having a Dream, but a reference to the Creation Period. Dreamtime is a manual for 'learning in the footsteps of the ancestors,' an oral scripture that recounts the world's beginnings while guiding social life, spiritual practice, relations between the sexes, and the responsibilities of every member of the community. Dreamtime is a collection of stories that encapsulates knowledge transmitted through art, song, and dance to children and teenagers who will later be initiated into the tribes' secrets. These stories represent their religion and the laws that govern their society and their lives.

One of the obligations that stems from Dreamtime is to leave on a Walkabout of the territory the Aboriginal people associate with themselves and maintain links with their Nation and their neighbors. Therefore, an Aboriginal person may decide one morning to leave on a Walkabout without anyone knowing where he is going or how long he will be gone, reestablishing the ties he is spiritually mandated to maintain, all to the despair of the rest of the population throughout the country who go to work every day, rhythmically, locking themselves in cubicles...

In their Walkabout, the Aborigines move across the continent on Dreaming Tracks, as they call them, which represent the paths followed by their ancestral creative spirits. By following these imaginary trails, the Aboriginal person retraces the path of the creators who passed along, through an exclusively oral tradition handed down through generations, the location of these spiritual places that have become part of the local ancestral memory and must be cherished and protected. During a Walkabout, Aboriginal people trace these tracks by singing a song in which they speak, in their own tongue, the words linked to the sacred sites they encounter. The song is unique, and its precise cadence is more important than the language in which it is sung. The words may vary from place to place along the pilgrimage, but the song itself remains unchanged. However, during the Walkabout, the words must be pronounced in a precise order; otherwise, the very creation of the place may be jeopardized. In this way, the Dreaming Tracks become Songlines that accompany the Aboriginal person on this initiatory journey. "Song and path are the same thing," said Chatwin.

An Aborigine who knows the songs of a place can travel great distances and cross the entire continent, making this journey to find a wife in a distant tribe, thus protecting himself from the taboo of incest. A person usually knows the song of his own territory and maybe three or four from neighboring lands. Completing his song signals that he has reached the edge of his territory. Yet what astonishes outsiders is that someone from a northern tribe, unfamiliar with the language of a southern tribe, can pinpoint its location just by listening to the song's melody, without comprehending a single word. Could it be that telepathy takes place while the Aborigines walk the Songlines in a trance? Tonality defines the location, assuming that the musical phrase itself describes the type of relief and shapes of a place. An Aboriginal on a Walkabout is engaging in a religious ritual. By singing the stanzas in their inherited order, he recreates the world as it was formed during Creation, acting as a guardian of tradition. In local belief, the Walkabout is mandatory, for land that is left unsung will die along with all its creation. The Songlines also confer a form of spiritual paternity on the individual. Along the tracks once traveled, the ancestors scattered spirit-names that continue to permeate the land. From infancy, the Songlines are imprinted on the Aboriginal's consciousness, with each child receiving a stanza at birth that defines his own space. Tradition claims that a pregnant woman who walks along the track at some point becomes spiritually impregnated by these child-spirits she encounters, giving the newborn the unique right to a particular stanza of the song linked to the place she passed.

"The song is the title deed of the place," writes Bruce Chatwin, "which the individual can neither escape nor sell." Not surprisingly, these tracks pass through places with waterholes and represent the continent's trade routes for a trade completely different from the one we understand today. Goods were exchanged for a dialog, and the exchanges were always equal, with objects not necessarily useful to the givers or the receivers. However, this exchange of goods created bonds and strengthened alliances.

CHAPTER 3

Sleeping Under the Stars

WE DIDN'T KNOW ANY SONGLINES WHEN WE ARRIVED in Alice Springs. But right after our 42-hour flight with many layovers, we went straight into our own Walkabout, followed by a swarm of annoying flies, to discover this miraculous world spiritually steeped in legends, which we found populated by completely different species of birds and animals than the ones we left behind. Flocks of parrots of various colors, shy wallabies who nonetheless stood to be photographed, and howling dingoes surrounded us. We roamed through a landscape that had changed little since the Englishmen arrived, except for a modern bicycle track leading into town.

The town of Alice Springs began as a mere dot on the map, its presence owed to a single water hole, that rarest of treasures in the desert. The location was named Stuart, after the first Englishman who led an expedition to the continent's center. Soon after, Colonel Todd and his wife Alice entered the scene. Alice, overwhelmed by the heat and annoyed by the flies, spent most of her time by the spring. She became such a fixture at the water hole that the new colonists eventually named the spring after her. In the end, the Adelaide bureaucrats, who always had in mind the watering hole more than the yet non-existent town, ended up changing the name in their books to Alice Springs, forgetting Stuart and his expedition.

Colonel Todd had been sent here by the British Empire to build a telegraph line linking the continent's north to its southern part. The 3,200-kilometer telegraph line from Darwin in the north to Port Augusta on its southern coast would later be connected using an underwater line to Java and thence to the rarefied heights of the Empire. Charles Todd was asked to build this line in this uncharted, barren terrain that he had to cross by camel. The camels brought to Australia by Afghans in 1860 became the vehicle for continental exploration, carrying Stuart on his double-crossing and then Colonel Todd in the construction of the telegraph line. If the British had ever ridden elephants in India, they might have found camels considerably more comfortable. In any case, it beats walking. However, the next century's cars forced the camels into retirement, and they were abandoned in the bush. Today, Australia faces a serious challenge with more than a million wild camels roaming the desert. Colonel Todd was required to complete the telegraph's construction in 18 months, which he managed to do by commissioning the installation in 1872. As I read this, I wondered how long it would take modern telephone companies to accomplish the same task under similar conditions. And only if the unions would approve… Situated in the heart of the continent, Alice Springs was designated as a telegraph hub. It started with a simple cabin and sleeping quarters for telegraphers, where Charles Todd became superintendent.

The story is fascinating, yet it resembles many accounts of how the English developed the lands they conquered despite seemingly insurmountable odds.

If the story of the telegraph is relatively interesting, what I found fascinating was the story of the flying doctors. The Royal Flying Doctor Service was founded in Alice Springs following a petition filed in 1911 by a reverend who sought to aid the pioneers settling in the Outback. The great distances made medical assistance almost impossible. People had to walk for days or ride in wagons over terrible roads or tracks in the wilderness, often destroyed by bad weather, with no chance of arriving in time to cure their illness. The petition requested a medical service using an airplane to reach people in the Outback facing urgent health emergencies. In 1928, after much debate, the Australian Parliament approved the establishment of the service, which continues to operate today with outstanding results, covering an area larger than all of Europe—from England to eastern Turkey. I couldn't help thinking as I listened to their story that almost a century after the founding of such a service in a forgotten corner of the world, right-wing American politicians try hard to eliminate the meager health insurance of a large part of the population in the richest country in the world.

However, the service was initially intended to aid only the English men and women who had settled in the Outback. Aborigines were and still are marginalized today. You see them walking like shadows outside the few streets that make up the city center. The knifing cases are numerous, giving Alice Springs the unenviable title of Australia's stabbing capital, forcing locals to take a taxi for even a few blocks if their destination isn't right downtown. What happened and how it all got this way is hard to say because the few Australians we asked about the situation of the Aboriginal people answered quite evasively: "It's actually kind of embarrassing, but we don't know anything about Aborigines."

We flew into Alice Springs to dive into this mysterious red Outback that we read a lot about, maybe a bit infatuated with Bruce Chatwin's stories, and mesmerized by those fabulous Songlines. A tight schedule caused by some business meetings in Sydney gave us only two nights in the desert, and to my utmost surprise and shock, no hotel rooms were available for those days. Not that there were many hotels at all. I started to fret and poked the Internet desperately looking for a solution, but the offers were quite murky. Finally, I found something that sounded weird but, in the end, turned out to be the only available option: sleep under the stars. What that actually meant was anyone's guess—maybe just some beds laid outside under a makeshift canopy. Their Mulga website—what the hell is that Mulga?—mentioned that everybody would sleep in swags. We had no clue what these swags might be because in America, the word refers to promotional clothing material given by a company. In the end, it is what it is because, in the Australian Outback, you can't expect too much comfort. So, we decided on the 'open stars' option despite a warning from someone who had just come from there who said: "You see, these Aussies are a bit rough, very different from us. You guys should take care". I doubted it though…

The plan was to join a small group for a six-hour drive to Uluru, the sacred rock of the Aboriginal people, deep in the heart of the Outback. The next morning, Matt stopped his camper van in front of our hotel at exactly 6 AM. On his T-shirt was printed the company logo: 'WTF's a Mulga?' But WTF do they mean by 'sleeping under the stars'? He stopped at several hotels in Alice Springs, loading up sleepy Westerners, each carrying a backpack and a sleeping bag, all as confused as we were about how things would turn out. Gradually, the sun came out, and with it, the shapes of the bush shrubs began to stand out more clearly, parading in front of the van like paralyzed dancers. The van sped along the flawless asphalt lane of the Stuart Highway, called by the locals 'The Track', which runs north to south across Australia, connecting Darwin with Adelaide on an almost 3000 km stretch.

The outback is huge. It is over 6 million square kilometers, almost twice the size of India, and while driving there's no reason to stop. Apart from the shrubs that spread as far as you could see, there were eucalyptus and mulga trees, a striking evergreen, many charred by occasional lightning, stretching for hundreds of kilometers. No large intersections could be seen except some red dirt roads leading to who knew where. You could imagine how desolate you might feel on such a road, lost in the red desert with no signal whatsoever, if even the traffic on the main thoroughfare of the continent seemed sparse. The asphalt strip going straight through the surrounding sea of red dirt seemed conquered by the 'truckies' who drove their large vehicles as if on automatic pilot, running over everything in their path. Local stories mentioned a man found flattened on the road, run over so many times it was thought to be a kangaroo. The muscular kangaroos are the main danger on the road, with the 'jumping kangaroo for the next 50 km' signs continuously lining the sides of the road. All cars, including our van, had a heavy grid in front to protect the driver in case of an impact with an oblivious jumping kangaroo, which may have sent many drivers to the hospital. However, we did not see even one, at least to take a picture of it!

The gas stations were few and far between, often separated by hours of driving. They each had a restaurant with a small shop, and the ones we stopped at were near a camel or an emu farm or had large cages filled with spectacularly colorful parrots and cockatoos. In this desolate landscape, the town of Erlanda seemed a burgeoning city with its car-repair garage next to a restaurant and a gas station. Here we turned onto Lasseter Highway, named for Harold Lasseter, the prospector whose ill-fated search for a legendary gold reef left its mark on Outback history. He is credited with discovering Uluru, setting aside the fact that the Aborigines had lived with it for millennia.

We continued our drive towards Australia's spiritual heartland, surrounded by the same bushes frozen in their malefic ballet, to Curtin Springs, the last pitstop for gas and food, with several gigantic cages filled with colorful parakeets and budgerigars. And finally, after the last segment of a road that seemed like it would never end, we found ourselves in front of the magnificent rock.

Uluru is spectacular in its singularity. A gigantic 364-metre-tall rock that rises unexpectedly from the Earth. Around it is just flat land with no other forms sticking out as far as you can see. It also has an interesting shape, as if it were a giant ship that had accidentally crash-landed into the surrounding wilderness, clad in a texture that in some places resembled an animal's skin sleeping out its eternity. Geologists classify Uluru as an inselberg, an island-like mountain measuring 10 km around. But in fact, the summit that emerges is part of a giant rock that lies underground over a vast area in the continent's center. The Englishman who discovered it named the monolith Ayers Rock after the secretary-general responsible for South Australia.

For the Anangu Aborigines, Uluru is one of the most sacred places in Australia, a place of legends at the crossroads of many Songlines. Around the rock are several springs, water holes, and caves, some of which have the walls covered in drawings. Stones taken from here are said to bring bad luck, and many tourists in search of souvenirs sent back, by FEDEX, large chunks of rock to break the curse that might have affected them or their household.

ULURU ROCK

In the local lore, Uluru emerged from the Earth as a result of a fight between two neighboring tribes of ancient spirits over a beautiful lizard woman. They fought fiercely, and both tribe chieftains were killed, covering the earth around them in their blood. The amount of blood shed made the earth rise in grief and created Uluru. Another legend puts the creation of Uluru on ancestral beings who traveled across the land. Uluru's caves, cliffs, and fissures are said to be imprints left by these spirits on the earth. But the caves are also linked to Tatji, the red lizard who, in a Dreamtime story, hurled a curved stick, or *kali,* at Uluru and then scooped out the rock with his hands, forming the bowl-shaped cavities. When walking around Uluru, it feels like the rock was scooped out in various places by giants, its smooth, slick surface opening up unexpectedly in sharp angles that look unnatural.

One of the larger caves hidden under a huge boulder is Mutitjulu, an Anangu family cave. Here, men brought venison, and the rest of the family gathered bush food. After which, all gathered around the table and told stories while eating. The cave's walls were painted with anthropomorphic and zoomorphic figures in a chromatic palette. The rock's undulating shape plunges towards the ground, resembling a frozen gigantic wave, arrested in its advancement towards an inexistent beach by an invisible force. Small rivulets of rainwater stream down the rock's surface, pooling into tiny mirrors at its base that reflect the white, puffy clouds above. Mai Tjuta is one of these waterholes, a place where the Aboriginal people left in Walkabout rest for several days.

Some places around Uluru have their own stories, like the one of Lungkata, who, traveling from Kata Tjuta, found an emu impaled by a spear. Hungry, Lungkata ate the bird and lied about it when the Panpanpalala hunters came searching for their prey. Enraged, the men chased him to his lair and lit a fire beneath it, the rising smoke choking him and forcing him to flee. As Lungkata rolled down the rock, strips of his burning flesh clung to the slick surface. With each turn, he grew smaller and smaller—until he finally transformed into a solitary stone.

On one side of Uluru, a steep trail marked by pylons and chains climbs to the top of the rock. For the Aborigines, the rock is sacred, but only recently has the government passed a law that prohibits ascent on the rock, applying heavy fines to those who defy the ban.

Uluru is a place of sacred initiation for Pitjantjatjara Anangu, the local Aboriginal people. In their hierarchical society, men's and women's affairs are entirely separate, each group keeping its own secrets and legends, with both protecting them from outsiders. The level of secrecy extended so far that photography of specific sites was forbidden, and even the nearby store offered no brochures or booklets. The sacred sites of initiation are very clearly identified in the tribe's traditional law. In Tjukurpa, the rock details and features represent no less than a divine scripture describing the cultural secrets known only by the tribe.

Certain caves were dedicated to the men participating in the initiation process, which are lairs of young eagles whose feathers are used in the ceremony. Other caves were assigned to wise elders and women. Here lies the legend of the Devil Dingo, the fierce canine who carried off *Naldawata,* the towering ceremonial pole known as the Kangaroo Tail, the very axis around which the elders once gathered. The Devil Dingo had been sung into existence by elders farther west in the mountains and sent into the camp at Uluru to punish the Mala group for refusing to supply eagle feathers to their cousins. This Devil Dingo forced everyone to flee, and the signs of their panic are still visible today in the writhe-marks left on the paw-shaped caves at the base of Uluru. In 1985, the Australian government returned the rock and the entire park to the Aboriginal people, who now manage the site and enforce their own rules.

We strolled around the rock, basking in the desert sunset that colored everything around it in a purple hue. Arriving in the evening at the campground where we were supposed to stay overnight, we all started to look around for comfortable beds, but nothing looked usable for sleeping. A large metal shed served as the camp's storeroom, equipped with a grill stove, a long table, and several benches. A bit further away, in contrast with the Spartan environment, were some spotless hot water showers and immaculate toilets, brightly lit in the crepuscular light.

In the storeroom, however, on top of some racks were those famous swags mentioned on the website, thin little mattresses encased in a thick, waterproof rubberized material. A flap meant to protect you from the rain could be pulled over the head and face. This was our hotel for the night, set directly on the ground, but right 'under the stars'. The contraption looked and felt just a touch cushier than a body bag, but once you stepped inside and closed the flap, from the outside, there was no hint of any life pulsing within the rubberized sarcophagus. Nobody other than one Australian couple who were part of the group had ever slept in anything like this, and you could see the panic etched on all Westerners' faces who didn't quite know what to do. As we learned in later conversations, most Aussies keep swags at home, and when they feel the need to be in contact with nature, they take them out of the cupboards and sleep in their yard, on the ground. Per Matt's instructions, we began searching for a flat spot on the ground with no stones or small pebbles, and we entered the flexible sarcophagus sprawled across the desert dust, all of us thinking of the venomous spiders and snakes that slither on the continent.

"No worries about snakes or scorpions," said Matt. "They won't bother your sleep, but if you have a tiny pebble by your ribs, that will keep you awake all night, so look carefully", a statement that made us all crawl again, pointing lanterns and phone lights towards the ground, inspecting its minuscule relief like we had lost a ring or an AirPod.

But all terrifying thoughts were dispelled as we lay on our backs and above us unfolded the southern sky with an explosion of stars twinkling like nowhere else, illuminating this lost corner of the world. The Milky Way was a giant continuous bright patch as if somebody, by accident, dropped a box of powdered milk over the sky's tapestry. Everything was so impressive that despite the fatigue induced by the jet lag, we didn't want to fall asleep. It was the most beautiful sky we had ever seen. Finally, exhausted, we fell asleep and awoke in the middle of the night under moonlight that hid the twinkling of the stars, casting a silvery veil over the entire landscape, from where howls of dingoes could be heard in the distance; a deluge of stars that accompanied and guided the Walkabout of the Aborigines for thousands of years and star lines that lit the tracks they followed on land as they hummed those magical Songlines. These were the same star lines that paradoxically helped the Englishmen who copied the Songlines of the Aborigines and built, parallel with them, the modern highways that crisscross the continent. In the morning, we woke up with a feeling of unbound joy, thinking that the next night we would sleep again under the stars.

Kata Tjuta is seen in the distance when you leave Uluru; a heap of giant rounded boulders tossed carelessly by the giant demiurge who created the songs of the place. Also called The Olgas after the name of Russia's Tsar Nicholas' daughter, married to King Charles of Württemberg, Kata Tjuta is a Pitjantjatjara word for 'many heads'. Legends describe Kata Tjuta as the home of the snake Wanambi, a demiurge of creation, who formed the rivers and springs, which sits coiled in a water hole atop the highest peak and only descends into the valley when the weather is dry. The strong wind we felt when we hiked through the Valley of the Winds is, in the local lore, the breath of the demiurgic serpent. Each formation has a legend: women mice, the kangaroo-man Malu held by his sister, the Pungalunga giants eating Aboriginal hunters and their families, one of the giants killed by a spear thrust in his back after it was found out that he ate the wife of one of the hunters. But most legends are kept secret, shared only within the tribe. Kata Tjuta is an important male-only initiation site where local women are forbidden even to visit.

We followed a several-kilometer track under the spectacular red cliffs of the Valley of the Winds, walking by huge boulders of conglomerate rocks and sporadic trees, and climbed up to a lookout point. The rocks above had staggered caves looking as if they were scooped out by a giant who wanted to climb a staircase to heaven, towards the top of the rounded peaks and command the region from there.

We continued on a winding trail at the base of the rocks, climbing a steep trail towards an opening between the rocks at the Karingana Lookout. At the base, the valley in front looked like a display of red eggs framed by the Olgas with traces of green splashes from its abundant vegetation. Though a desert, this region is remarkably abundant in life, with tens of species of animals and birds and hundreds of species of native plants. The hike was over, and on the way to the new campsite where we were supposed to spend the night 'under the stars', we picked dry mulga wood for a campfire around which we ate kangaroo steaks and camel burgers, holding sticks with marshmallows by the fire. There are few chances of eating vegan in Australia... We went to our now familiar swags in the last flickers of the fire, all gathered radially around the hearth, with the same mesmerizing spectacle of the Southern Cross above us, and fell asleep amid the rustles of camels that were grazing somewhere nearby, perhaps as fascinated as we were by the same sky spectacle.

In the morning, we all woke up with a sense of loss. This was the last day in the Outback, and in the afternoon, we would fly to the coast. We wished we had another night sleeping in swags under the shimmering stars, but 'that was all, folks'. The group we had joined included travelers from eight European countries, the USA, and Australia, and everyone seemed to relish the unexpected adventure. They shared their stories over meals, helping Matt, who couldn't cook alone, and chatting in a jovial atmosphere as if they had known each other for years.

After the last breakfast together, we packed and went for a hike in Watarrka National Park. The hike was on the rim of Kings Canyon, soaring a hundred meters above Kings Creek to a plateau of rocky domes. We climbed about 350 steps through a red rock landscape reminiscent of Utah's spectacular pancaked dome formations. Domes after domes, an entire landscape formed only by these red mounds as far as you could see. The canyon is well known in Australia as the background of a famous local movie shot here. Staircases lead to the heights, passing through Priscilla's Crack and reaching a stunning spot nicknamed the Garden of Eden, where light reflecting off the red rock casts magical hues on the water below.

From there, you climb atop the canyon, walking on surfaces that resemble petrified undulating dunes, frozen in their march by powerful winds. Ahead, we could see a perfectly flat vertical face of the canyon, seemingly cut by a gigantic knife—a ceremonial site for the local Aboriginal people. The six-kilometer hike around the rim of this extraordinary chasm offers a view of the canyon in all its glory. Descending from the rim towards the canyon base, we passed through a forest of scattered trees behind which hid waterholes, places where perhaps an Ancestral Being morphed into the landscape. We were still lost in the magic of the desert when we were awakened to reality; the van was in the parking place, and Matt was ready to take us to the airport, where the plane was waiting on the tarmac. The story was over. If only we had been able to buy a swag and pack inside the sky full of stars under which we slept, imagining for a moment that we became just a speck among the local legends.

CHAPTER 4

STAYIN' ALIVE

"YOU HAVE TO TAKE CARE DOWN THERE," WE WERE TOLD numerous times when we said we'd go to Australia. We heard anecdotal stories about the venomous snakes and spiders on the continent, but we did not pay much attention to the warnings. But when we read the *Dangers and Annoyances* box in the Lonely Planet guide of Australia detailing the many ways in which you can die there, we were wondering if we could make it back. It felt like everything in Australia was lurking in the background, plotting against us—except for the people, who turned out to be the absolute champions of laid-back vibes. So naturally, *Stayin' Alive,* that classic Bee Gees anthem, became our unofficial travel motto as we navigated the land down under!

And it took almost no time to have our first encounter. Just after we dropped our luggage at the Alice Springs hotel and headed out for a casual hike beyond town surrounded by flocks of colorful parrots that tried to distract our attention from the annoyances of the flies, we ran into something we absolutely had not expected. We passed a small shop, and while chatting with the friendly owner she proudly showed us a photo on her phone: a pack of dingoes.

"They were hanging out right here," she said cheerfully. "If you're lucky, you can see them. They're so cute. You'll see…"

Cute is not exactly the word I would use for a pack of wild dogs—rebranded as dingoes—especially if they happen to be hungry and considering whether to add us to their bespoke chef's menu. Having had my fair share of encounters with vicious shepherd dogs while hiking in Romania, I knew one thing for sure: distance is your friend. I had even been forced to learn a few techniques for dealing with them, but somehow, I doubted that faking an Australian shepherd's accent—whatever that might sound like—would help much here. These were wild. Pure wild. *Cute* in a photo, perhaps, while sipping a latte in an AC cafe. In real life, not so much.

Naturally, once the idea was planted, we became mildly obsessed with the possibility of meeting them. And sure enough, as we hiked out of town, we saw something ahead on the trail—a tail, disappearing swiftly into the bush.

Oh, my…. Should we chicken out and turn back now, or keep going?

As we stood there debating, a voice called out not far away:

"Oscar… Oscar…"

I assumed someone was calling a child, a brother, maybe a friend lost in the bush. But as the trail approached a road, the calls grew louder, and soon we spotted a man cruising slowly in a convertible. He stopped shouting when he saw us.

"Hey, mate. By any chance did you see my dog?"

"Your *dog*?!"

"Yeah. He ran off. I'm pretty sure he went to hang out with the dingoes. There's a pack around here, and he loves playing with them. Listen! You can hear them."

We went quiet. And then we heard it—the howling, drifting up from somewhere in the valley lost somewhere in the sunset. Not too close, thankfully, but close enough. It was the sound of wild Australia as imagined: ancient, eerie, and utterly unconcerned with our survival.

"Well," I said carefully, "we may have seen your Oscar. Just his tail vanishing into the bush. He was right in front of us on the trail and were wondering if that was the "derriere" of one of the dingoes. It honestly freaked us out."

"Oh really? Great!" he said, genuinely pleased. "He's young, though, and they might ruffle him up a bit. I don't like it when he disappears like this."

"Oscar… Oscaaaar!" he resumed yelling.

At that point, we decided it was best to leave before Oscar found his friends and they all came trotting over together. We turned back toward Alice Springs, this time sticking firmly to the bike path—adding at least a symbolic layer of civilization between us and the wilderness.

Surely, none of the perils Australia is known for were breaking news; they had lingered for centuries in the rich tapestry of Aboriginal myth. According to their traditions, in waterholes, riverbeds, and swamps lived a man-eating mythical monster known by a local tribe as Bunyip, who hunts women and children by night and eats them. Also, in the Hawkesbury River lurks the Hawkesbury River Monster known as Mooney Mooney, a monstrously tall eel. Quite powerful, it can capsize canoes with a single thrust and, with its hypnotic gaze, ensnare its victims, submerging them beneath the waves. The Aboriginals revere him as a guardian of sacred sites and a conduit between realms, connecting the outside world with the realm of ancestors.

On land, you may be attacked by a carnivorous bear that lives in trees and drops down onto unsuspecting campers. Fig trees are also dangerous because on their branches lives Yara-ma-yha-who, a small red man with a large head. He plunges from the tree onto unsuspecting victims and sucks their blood, weakening them before swallowing them entirely. If you manage to escape these monsters, you then have to watch out for the Yowie, a hairy, bipedal creature said to inhabit remote parts of Australia, but is perceived by the local tribes as a spirit that roams the earth at night. The term 'yowie' may be an alteration of the Aboriginal word *yahoo*. Well, it's an evil spirit and not a famous search engine.

There is also the Rainbow Serpent, a mythical creature that appears in the Dreaming of many Aboriginal groups in Australia and is depicted in 7,000-year-old rock cave paintings. An important Aboriginal deity, the serpent, is both a creator and destroyer of life, a protector of the land, and a source of all life, which brings rain and causes floods, but also lords over fertility aspects, for both nature and women. As a guarantor of the social norms, the Rainbow Serpent teaches man how to live in the desert and create societies, punishing those who trespass on its norms. If you read about these myths, you might think there was a good reason the Aboriginals created them. Yet none of them made it into that frightening section of the Lonely Planet.

The first—and perhaps the easiest—challenge was driving on the wrong side of the road. Sorry, I meant to say the left side. Wherever they stayed, these Brits managed to throw the traffic into chaos. And, of course, they pretend they are the right ones, and we, the clueless ones, drive on the wrong side of the road. Besides, they built roads with roundabouts at every corner, which might make you think the Aussies hate straight lines. Cars were coming from all directions, the ones behind us probably wondering what we were waiting for to drive into the circle. But somehow, we were able to follow the flow and made it in one piece to the other side.

When you drive through the Outback, you see the jumping kangaroo, a sign on the side of the road, beneath which is written 'the next 50 km. The muscular animal poses a real danger to small cars and vans, all of which are fitted with metal grids—like shields—at the front to protect occupants in case of an unexpected collision.

We may have been lucky in the Outback, sleeping on the ground in swags. But when we felt only a thin layer between the ground and our body, we could not avoid thinking about the Australian snakes, some of the most venomous on the planet. Being in the middle of the continent, we could not know if we were bitten by an eastern or a western brown snake, but it probably would not have made a difference. Dead is dead… But if the snakes spared us, nobody would have protected us from one of the crawling spiders, one of the 520 species that Australia has. It could have been either the red-back spider, the mouse spider, or the wolf spider, not to mention the funnel spider, considered the most venomous in the galaxy, if spiders were invented in other solar systems. And just for fun, to make the horror more intense, we also read about the giant centipedes that grow to more than six inches and have, guess what, thousands of legs that move haphazardly, terrifying the victim, in this case, us. There are also the Australian paralysis ticks, practically undetectable, whose fun is to latch onto humans and inject proteins from the tick's saliva that create a lethal allergic reaction in the entire body. But the jetlag crushed us, and if any of these crawlers were around, for sure they would have feasted on us. But we fell asleep right away and woke up, alive and even refreshed, in the middle of the spectacular night sky lit by zillions of stars, waking up again in the morning and still kicking. In the end, we made it; 'Stayin' Alive' in the Outback.

Protected by fate, we decided to change the landscape and traveled by plane over the red dirt of Australia's central heartland. We eventually got tired and started to doze, just to wake up when we were descending upon the most verdant place we had ever seen: Cairns on the eastern coast of Australia. From there, a small drive brought us to Port Douglas, a charming town where the people are even more relaxed than all the other Aussies, if this is even possible. The entire coast is a tourist playground. Fast boats take hordes of tourists every day to the Great Barrier Reef, where they dive with colored fish that swim lazily among colorful and beautifully shaped corals. Parts of the reef were dead, but the large majority was spectacular.

And here were the famous Australian jellyfish. Of course, jellyfish are everywhere, in all seas, and many swimmers get stung by them. But not by the Aussie jellyfish that, of course, can be no other way than deadly. They invade the waters, forcing the beaches to close in full season. These are the Blue Bottle jellyfish. But what do they mean by bottle? I think they carry a canister of venom, and when frustrated, they unleash it on rosy-skinned Brits, Germans, and French, ready for a swim. The danger is so high that each Australian beach has a vinegar station, marked clearly at its entrance. Because when you get stung and run like a lunatic to put as much distance between you and the transparent blue creatures, your only chance is to stop on the way to the hospital by the vinegar station to spread some of the liquid on your wounds to alleviate the excruciating pain. But no matter what, you must continue to the hospital for real treatment. To protect its divers, the Great Barrier Reef tours outfit everyone in neoprene wetsuits and provide each person with a child's pool float. It's pretty nice and very colorful otherwise. Wrapped in these swimsuits, we felt somewhat protected, so the only concern was not to get cut by stepping on corals or worse, on a stonefish with its zillion spines that flood your bloodstream with venom, making you feel that you were hit over the entire body by a hammer. It elicits such pain in the body that the person may die from shock. The creature sits still on the underwater rocks and, to piss you off, it may live even outside in the atmosphere for up to 24 hours. Of course, these were more than enough, so we didn't even bother to think about the sharks. The Aussies say just swim with them, and they may go away. Or they may not and then…

But Port Douglas was so quaint that you could not even imagine that a few steps out of town, all these dangers were looming over you and your vacation. The docks were full of tourists, and we chatted with both locals and some Californians who decided to move here because the rhythm was for sure more paced than in the beach towns of their sunny state. If they feel like that about their life rhythm, what could a New Yorker say?

The crocodiles we discovered the next day were the apotheosis of hell. And they were just the freshwater crocs, not the gigantic saltwater ones that live in the waters of the Northern Territories. We saw them while on a boat going to Daintree Forest, the only rainforest that reaches the ocean. We went to see the crocs, since the only ferry over the Daintree River, the fragile link between Cape Tribulation and the rest of Australia, had broken down again—much to the despair of the locals, who had only fixed it four months before. If you look at a six-foot croc lying on the sand, you might think that it is lazily sleeping, but if you just touch the water, it may jump like a spring and gulp you in one piece. What seemed even more menacing was when we found out that on the ground, a croc would run at the same speed as a man. The only chance to get away would be to run in a zig-zag because the croc cannot move its tail. But tell me sincerely, would you bet on that? How about a yoga croc that could bend easily?

Eventually, after we saw an entire display of crocs on the dunes and our ferry started to disperse the cars, we entered the green tunnel of the tropical forest, driving carefully not to hit a cassowary. The national bird of Australia is a piece of work. It is a funny-looking flightless bird, a combination of an ostrich and a turkey. The creature is a pissed-off bird that would overrun you easily and attack you with dagger-like nails that grow on two of their six toes. The birds attack several clueless tourists each year, but rarely does someone get killed. The entire road is marked with signs alerting tourists to the possible encounter, but the forest held them at bay, allowing us to continue walking the beautiful boardwalks under large palm fronds and rainforest plants, all looking like in an *Indiana Jones* movie, without the lost temple.

Along the way to Cape Tribulation, the beaches were spectacular; empty stretches of silvery sand, untouched by human feet, with palm trees leaning over the beach, on idyllic gulfs that you could see only in the movies. We walked on along these empty beaches, trying to reach their ends, and did not encounter anyone. Why was nobody on the beach in this corner of paradise, we wondered?

The answer came when we read what was written on a board impaled in the sand:

'Don't come closer than 10 feet from the seashore' because the nicely sunbathing freshwater crocs may come to say 'Hi' to you. Lazing all day on the river's beach and looking for food or maybe getting bored out of their minds, the crocs adapted to saltwater, where they go for a swim in the sea towards the next freshwater estuary. And on the way, if you want to offer yourself for lunch, they would not refuse. So, we turned around and left the paradisiacal empty beach, passing by the jellyfish vinegar station, which we perceived more indulgently.

When we thought that we had finally exhausted all the possible menaces looming over us, our path was crossed by a five-foot monitor lizard. Of course, it's just a lizard and is vegetarian or even vegan. But when you walk peacefully with no worries, and this five-footer just shows up in front, you feel that you stepped straight into Jurassic Park.

"There are only four of them, and they are harmless," one of the rangers from Cape Tribulation Park told us. "But don't chase them in the forest because they will attack and bite you". Even the vegans bite in Australia, for God's sake!

We drove back to Cairns and hopped on a plane to Sydney, determined to put as much distance as possible between ourselves and Australia's never-ending lineup of deadly menaces. At the hotel, we went straight to the pool for much-needed relaxation. But wait—what's that? Something was moving on the other side of the water. Oh no… Not again! Bracing ourselves for another Australian weirdness, we cautiously got out. We tiptoed around the pool's edge, only to find a harmless plastic clownfish, probably left behind by a child, lazily bobbing up and down with the ripples. Relieved but still on edge, we finally relaxed, haunted only by the thought that mythical creatures might enter the pool water systems and hang out at business hotels in their downtime.

CHAPTER 5

OH, THOSE AUSSIES

IT WAS A SUNNY DAY OF A GLORIOUS FALL. CROWDS were out strolling in Bryant Park, in the heart of Manhattan, stopping by the tiny tables to eat lunch or have a coffee. The tourists looked chill, taking their time for selfies or having an animated chat while looking around at all the others rushing to their offices after a short break. A lot of work was waiting for those guys, and they had to finish it. Today. Or even yesterday, if that could be arranged. I was not one of them, neither a tourist nor somebody who had to go to the office. I sat down at a table with my latte, put my laptop on the table, took a book out of my backpack, and started to read. Or rather, I was trying to read despite the loud conversation at a nearby table, which kept pulling my attention away. A guy standing was talking to a girl sitting at a table, telling her about New York: history, transportation, movies, work, mob, craziness, and even the Unabomber. The guy was speaking in an animated, loud voice, and I couldn't help eavesdropping. The girl was from Berlin, where she was studying in a PhD program, and was visiting New York for a collaboration at New York University. At one point, the guy left, and I was able to return to my book. But surprisingly, at one point, the girl turned to me, asking what I was reading. We started chatting about the book, democracy—the book's subject—in Europe and America, Trump, and, in the end, about New York, how she liked being here, how she found the city, its people.

"It's a great city, but I have no idea how you guys can live here," she said and continued. "It feels like insane stress living in a high-octane flow. I don't think I could withstand this crazy rhythm of life."

I was not surprised, as I have heard this before. But many European visitors, relatives, and friends were dismayed by the city's pulse. "You are so busy here" was what most of them said in various ways. And for good reason, because in New York, you feel that there is always something on your plate, something to do, and the feeling is that this had to be done yesterday or last week. You feel that time flows ahead of you and there's no chance to catch your breath. It whispers in your ear, telling you that you are already late to the game, even if the game has not even started.

"So, do you plan to stay here for a while or return to Berlin?" I asked.

"I have to spend some time here for this assignment at NYU, but I will return. Life is way more relaxed in Germany, or Europe in general. I love my four-week vacation and don't want to lose that," she finished with a smile.

I felt like this each time I traveled to Europe and many other places, most recently in Australia. I could count a few places in the developed world, especially competitive Anglo-Saxon countries, that would come even close to Australia's relaxed attitude toward the locals. A continent-country that lives its existence in an easygoing way that New Yorkers can hardly even dream of. Life in Australia happens at the pace of the 1960s in California. People move through their day with calm and ease, and a lingering look can easily lead to a conversation that stretches for an hour. It may happen on a train, passing through a small town and asking a question, or even in hectic Melbourne, where a guy working on a city project started to talk to me about the map I had in my hand. The next thing I knew was that I couldn't extract myself from a full hour of in-depth conversation about various topics, including Melbourne, its university, where he was a professor, and Australia in general. People are always eager to help in a way hardly encountered in many other places. Wherever I went, no one appeared to be in any rush. Ask a couple who seem deeply engaged in a business conversation to take your picture, and not only will they pause their discussion and happily oblige, but they might even strike up a friendly chat with you, apparently completely forgetting whatever they were talking about before. You see people sitting in cafes sipping cappuccinos and reading books. On any weekday around 5 p.m., crowds of Aussies fill up the bars, grabbing a drink and a delicious, heated snack. Others join large groups of friends and congregate in restaurants that serve refined dinners. Nightlife peaks on Saturday, with bars and clubs buzzing at full energy until the early hours, with music blasting onto the streets and cocktails flowing by the bar. And no matter what exciting things may be on your travel agenda, this relaxed spirit of the locals makes a place memorable like nothing else. You may forget where you have seen a specific view or a site, or the monuments and buildings may get mixed up in your mind, but you would hardly forget the spirit of the place where you dive into the soul of their inhabitants.

At first, Australia reminded me of America before 9/11. A terrorism-free country where almost no serious security issue happens. At the airport, you are whisked through with the water bottle and the shoes, and without passport checking, as long as you have a ticket on your phone. When we entered the La Boheme opera performance in Sydney's harbor, and opened our backpacks, the usher was puzzled and asked us what we wanted to show him because all he wanted was to see our tickets. You may see the occasional large cement flower pots that block a large building entrance, but otherwise, the only time we were made aware that threats might exist in the world was in the email we got from United Airlines for our return to the USA. In rest, quietude, and peacefulness.

One of the reasons the country is secure is because of a very tightly controlled immigration policy. No illegal immigration can happen on the sea because, according to the latest laws, if anybody tries to enter Australia illegally, they are automatically deported to Nauru, an offshore island, with the promise that they will never be allowed to step into Australia again. The living conditions on that island are so abysmal that even the Australian press is not allowed to report from there, to the outcry of the rights groups in the country. As a result of this rule and another racially based policy instituted at the beginning of the 20th century that lasted for 75 years, Australia looks like a white nation. Introduced in 1901, the White Australia policy gave preferential treatment to British migrants for its first forty years, before softening after the Second World War to admit migrants from other Christian countries. Adding to the predominantly white population, most tourists visiting Australia come from Europe and the USA, further reinforcing the sense of a privileged nation.

At the same time, in the middle of the continent, we could see the Aboriginal people moving almost like shadows on the outskirts of Alice Springs. The tensions simmering in the Aboriginal communities, ridden with alcoholism and drug abuse, often bring fights ending in stabbings. Rarely might it happen that a white person would be stabbed, but in order not to risk an encounter, the local whites take a taxi home even if it is just a five-minute walk. We asked many white Australians about their relationships with the Aboriginal people, and we rarely were able to get any answers. Many told us that they do not know the situation, and others mentioned the enormous amount of money poured by the government into the Aboriginal communities, schools, housing, and hospital development, just to be shunned by those who still prefer to live close to their sacred sites, undisturbed by civilization. There were also still people in the bush who found out only several decades ago that the 'whites' came to Australia. The Aborigines were able to preserve their traditions, which are manifested through their art, which is not the trade of a group of people, but it's the way their society lives and breathes. Art has long been a vital part of Aboriginal cultures, embodying the sacred essence of their world. A world that, according to their tradition, started at the Dreamtime.

This tension between preserving tradition and embracing modernity is not new; it began with the arrival of the British in Australia, and many solutions were attempted. One of the most devastating was the removal of Aboriginal children from their families and having them raised by British families, a thing that was done all over Australia, and raised much resentment. Nowadays, this policy and its moment in history are condemned, even though many of the current leaders of the

Aboriginal communities, as it is whispered, come from this milieu of British-raised children.

The relaxed state of mind of the Aussies also stems from other enlightened policies. After the large mass shooting of 1995 in Tasmania's Port Arthur, the government began a buy-back for all the nation's guns. Today, if you own a gun, you have to prove why you need it; otherwise, you have to give it back. The program cost the government a great deal of money and triggered numerous disputes with more independent regions such as Western Australia and the Northern Territories, but in the end, it brought peace to the nation.

"America is a sick nation with your gun laws. But you refuse to accept it," said one Aussie we met on the way. "It is a national malaise that your politicians, in cahoots with gun lobbies, refuse to cure". The man was following in dismay, like many others around the world, America's mass shootings and its sold-out politicians who, smiling, state that 'Guns don't kill people. People kill people.'

Higher education in Australia is emphatically supported by the government, which introduced college admission based on high school grades. For decades, college education was free, but more recently, universities introduced a low-tuition system tied to the projected income of graduates' specialties. The loan begins to be paid after graduation, only when the graduate reaches a specific plateau of projected earnings. In most cases, the loan, negligible compared to American standards, would be cleared in just three or four years.

In the 1980s, the government adopted a national health insurance policy that every Aussie we spoke with seemed to cherish. The policy was added to their impressive Royal Flying Doctor service, which was proposed and implemented in 1911 to serve people in the Outback, who were far away from medical services. And it happened that, by accident, we needed access to this medical system.

Cristina sprained her ankle. She walked to the Sydney office, tripped, and sprained her ankle right in front of the building. She limped to the office, stayed there for about two hours, and took a cab back to the hotel that was in close vicinity. When I came into the room, I found her with a swollen ankle as purple as an eggplant. Was anything broken? Her ankle hurt badly, and the only option was to go to a hospital. We had never considered this possibility before and had no idea whether, or how, our insurance would cover us in Australia. We fathomed a long and arduous experience in a country with socialized medicine. We pictured ourselves waiting in line for hours, uncertain whether anyone would even see her that night. Would they accept our insurance? Actually, why should they take it? Accustomed to the American system, I knew that visits and treatments—including the emergency room, an X-ray, an MRI, or a CAT scan—would cost a fortune. But in any case, there was nothing else to do. She could not put her foot on the ground, and the pain was excruciating, so we hopped in a cab that left us in front of the emergency room of a hospital in central Sydney. And now the wait... I brought my laptop and a book to keep myself occupied while waiting. How many hours? I could not even imagine.

No one was in the waiting room, and the nurse tending the reception desk invited us inside. Of course, we thought that we were lucky to find the emergency room waiting area in Sydney empty, while in New York, it is always full to the brim. The nurse took notes and mentioned something about 'a hundred dollars' for an X-ray. We thought we did not understand.

"What did she say? What was this for? No way. This is just the beginning. It will add up", I said, "and what did she ask you? What is your religion? Why should she ask about a thing like that? These guys know nothing about privacy. Maybe you don't want to say it, or you are an atheist. Anyway, whatever, let's go and wait because it will be hours until they take you," I continued.

We sat on a nearby couch, Cristina with her pain, and I pulled out my computer. "Cristina?" A nurse came out and asked us to come inside. I packed my computer and helped Cristina hop into the emergency room. The nurse set up a chair and began asking her questions that I was convinced were for the insurance paperwork. After that, I imagined that they would send us to wait for a long time in the lobby. Hours, or maybe a day, a week... Who knows? But the nurse was simply trying to understand what had happened and to document it. She mentioned the X-ray, and a radiologist came in asking me to help Cristina go to the room behind to take the radiography. In this socialized medicine system, the X-ray was finished 15 minutes after we were out of the cab.

Now, helped into a wheelchair by the radiologist, the medical personnel surrounding Cristina were joined by a young girl, who turned out to be the orthopedic doctor who began to consult her right away behind a curtain. She looked at the X-ray and concluded nothing was broken, just sprained ligaments. The young doctor wrapped her foot with some bands to remove the tension and left to file the paperwork. She returned with the X-ray loaded on a CD, while another nurse wrapped Cristina's foot in a tight sock. Two hours after we left the hotel room, we were told we were ready to go. The total cost came to about two hundred dollars.

"Incredible! And this is a socialized medicine system compared with our bloated system in the USA," Cristina said and continued:

"Do you remember when Victor (our son) got sick in Vegas and we went to the emergency room of that top Vegas hospital? We waited three hours just for a doctor to see him". I remember waiting for hours only to get confirmation of something we already knew: that he had the flu…

"They did not have to take any X-ray, and no procedures were done, but the copayment was as high as my entire visit to this hospital in Australia, which was completely out of pocket".

We have many bones to pick with health insurance in America, a country where if you have money, you have insurance. If you don't, you are a loser because, according to a part of our Congress's political spectrum, paradoxically, the ones who pretend to be the preservers of the Christian belief and morality, poor people are poor because of themselves.

And you still may wonder why these Aussies are so relaxed?

The Berlin girl got up and packed her laptop.

"I have to leave. I have a meeting at NYU in the afternoon. But it was nice talking to you…" She paused for a bit. "But, tell me, was it always like this? This intense pace?" she asked.

"Maybe not, but it's hard to gauge. In any case, now it is better than before the pandemic. The remote work helped, and this is a city where many jobs can be done remotely…" I said, pointing to my laptop connected to an office server.

She stood for a while trying to grasp my explanation.

"Here, you feel this palpable energy on the streets. But it doesn't seem to have a lull and becomes tiring after a while. I woke up last night after midnight, and the traffic was zooming under my window like it was midday. I thought that something had happened and looked out the window, but it seemed nothing out of the ordinary. You need a break from all this, and I don't know where you can escape to find that break. I still prefer Berlin..." and she disappeared into the crowded park.

CHAPTER 6

'That Nice Road'

"IT'S A NICE ROAD THERE", "NOT A LOT TO SEE, I HEARD, but the coastal road is very nice", "Yeah, that road from Hobart is worth a trip". This is all I had been able to find out when I asked people what they knew about Tasmania. And those I asked were transplanted Aussies in the USA who had never visited the island. Years ago, while traveling in Australia, I had heard about 'that nice road' in Tasmania, and it never seemed that you needed more than a few days to see everything. So, I began reading several articles, and the more I read, the more it piqued my interest, increasing the number of days planned to spend on the island. I started with several days, and it soon went up to a week. Or perhaps two weeks, with a few days spent in Australia? And so, after three flights and thirty-four hours, I finally landed in Hobart to look for 'that nice road'.

So, what is Tasmania really like? Picture this: an island in the Southern Hemisphere, where the ocean's waves break against rugged shores, surrounded by a thousand smaller islands with half a million inhabitants, nearly half of them living in Hobart, Tasmania's capital. Its story goes back 11,700 years when rising sea levels created the Bass Strait, isolating Tasmania from mainland Australia. The historical facts were etched in the legends of the Palawa people, the Aboriginal population of the island, who called this place home for about 42,000 years. Their legends are considered the oldest recorded stories in the world. The Palawa believed that the 'first man', named Parlevar, was shaped by the creation spirit Moinee from a kangaroo, known as Tarner. According to their tradition, all spirits live in stars, and the bright star Moinee was mentioned in the Palawa legends of the flood that submerged the land bridge connecting present-day Tasmania to Australia. Like many First Nation cultures, the Palawa have a legend of the Seven Sisters, seven young women chased by a male figure, represented by the Pleiades star constellation that traveled through time into Greek mythology.

Fast forward to 1803. Here came the Brits, and by 1825, they turned the island into a penal colony, shipping over 80,000 convicts within the next 30 years, to places like Port Arthur and Macquarie Harbor, both infamous for their harsh conditions. Tasmania's indigenous population, estimated between 3,000 and 7,000 at the Brits' arrival, dwindled drastically during what was called locally the Black War that lasted for the next six years. The brutal conflict saw desperate Aboriginal inhabitants clashing with settlers, partly driven by hunger but mainly by the abduction of their women and girls. The settlers had a severe gender imbalance—four men for every woman—and this imbalance was much higher among the inmates.

The violence only stopped in 1832 when the remaining Indigenous people were moved to Flinders Island, where many succumbed to diseases. This past gender imbalance, its low population with hints of inbreeding, and its penal history made Tassie, as Tasmania is affectionately called, the butt of jokes and stereotypes in Australia to the point that some mainlanders have even suggested the secession of the island to improve Australia's image.

Tasmania's modern history was profoundly shaped by its convict past, traces of which remain across the island. Not far from Hobart, on the Tasman Peninsula, lies Port Arthur, the notorious penal settlement. The convicts sent here were repeat offenders, but most of their offenses were petty crimes committed out of poverty and lack of opportunity. Once arrived in Port Arthur, for many of them, the detention morphed practically into a death sentence. The Victorian British Empire decided to teach all the inmates a trade to help them become useful members of society. The prison was turned into a factory, where the skills taught to inmates were put to work producing goods for the Empire. In its early days, the convict colony was overseen by commanding officers committed to improving the lives of the inmates. Over time, career-minded officers used the prison as a ladder to advancement, supplementing their income by covertly selling the goods produced by the prisoners for the empire. And because this was a white-collar crime, even if they got caught, nothing much happened to them except a note in the history books. Like today...

The prison was a vast complex that, in addition to the imposing convict building, included housing for officers and their families, a full garrison for defense, numerous workshops for manufacturing goods, as well as a church, post office, hospital, and all the typical facilities of a functioning town. The only difference was that the inhabitants were convicts, and most of them ended up buried here.

WOMBATS IN MARIA ISLAND, TASMANIA

Another convict colony in Tasmania was Maria Island. The island, just a short boat ride from Tasmania's coast, was originally inhabited by the Aboriginal people of the Tyrendemere tribe. Later, convicts were moved here, living and working on the island in two periods during the first half of the 19th century. Several silk and wine enterprises were set up here, benefiting from the same convict work. The island was also the gulag of its time for the Irish nationalists who participated in the Young Ireland Rebellion of 1848, fighting for Ireland's independence. Remnants of the structures from those times are scattered across the island and mainly preserved in the tiny hamlet of Darlington, the only settlement where you can rent a bike for exploring the island if you are not ready for a hike.

But the island is not visited for these ruins, but for the presence of all the endemic animals of Australia. Hiking the island's trails from the Painted Cliffs to the Fossil Cliffs, you bump into hopping kangaroos, shy wallabies, tiny padymelons, and unfazed wombats not bothered by the tourist attention that surrounds them with lots of cameras while grazing. They keep minding their business, and if the camera is in the way when the wombats walk toward their burrow, they bump it away and continue to their hole in the ground.

When I arrived in Hobart, the first thing that struck me was the silence. I strolled on streets lined with houses with charming courtyards full of flowers, and I could not hear a whisper. It seemed that everybody was sleeping. Even in the small corner parks, people were quietly sitting on the grass reading or walking their dogs in silence, with no words and no barking. Except for the city center, where a few tourists—mostly Australians—wandered, the side streets were empty. Hobart seemed the epitome of calm, a remote realm shielded from mass tourism by some invisible cloak, yet discovered almost by accident by independent travelers and hikers parading through town with backpacks bulging with sleeping bags and tents. Even if I saw a few tourist buses, they were so rare that I treated them like accidental holes in the magic mantle, leaving me with the impression that mass tourism is completely oblivious about this place.

The relaxed atmosphere extended to restaurants that closed their kitchens around 7:30 pm, and the risk of eating snacks for dinner was quite high if you did not make plans to arrive on time. I felt safe walking anywhere at any hour of the night. The only crime the city might be known for would be the white-collar variety, committed in its financial institutions. In the morning, the cafes opened early and the locals hung out having breakfast and chatting in the caressing sun, while others walked relaxed on Hobart's streets going to work. Stores and tourist places closed around 4 pm, and everybody seemed to enjoy this lifestyle, going out to chill with friends or head home, minding their own business, because tomorrow would be another day. All of it contributed to a warm, inviting aura, with cheerful and polite residents who seemed to greet everyone with a smile.

And if I asked a person on the street something, I always ended up engaged in a longer conversation about my trip, as if people here had all the time in the world to chat. And while in Hobart, the first thing they would say to me was that I must visit MONA. Although I had barely heard about this place and it did not make it to my list of top places to visit, the locals I spoke with kept insisting and convinced me to go there.

If MONA seems confusing, don't worry, it's meant to be this way. A spectacular architectural and artistic effort, it is a museum cut deep into the underground. MONA is the brainchild of David Shawn, a local dude who became a highly successful gambler—so successful, in fact, that he and his syndicate were banned from all casinos for consistently betting against the house and winning. David Shawn, with his long grey hair and unconventional dress, pretends to be on the autism spectrum, which, according to him, gave him an ease with numbers. Whether through his autistic intuition or card-counting skills, he made millions in all kinds of bets, from cards to horse races.

Yet at one point, he had an epiphany: everything he had done in life felt meaningless and senseless. So, he decided that the best thing to do was to start giving back part of the gambling winnings to his community in Hobart and came up with the brilliant idea of creating a museum that would collect remarkable works of art. MONA stands for Museum of Old and New Art, but its main theme is Sex and Death. According to David's statement, this was not the theme he chose, but was the theme that chose him through the work of contemporary artists obsessed with these two aspects of life. Today, his art collection numbers over 3,000 works. To showcase part of it, he created a spectacular underground building—two floors carved into the rock, filled with art of every kind. None of the pieces has a label. Instead, an app on your phone displays information about the artworks in each room as you enter. There is no museum map, leaving it to visitors to explore and discover remarkable pieces on their own—and it's far from obvious. To make access easier, a boat runs several times a day from Hobart, carrying visitors—and more art—across the water. The museum operates at a loss despite ticket revenue, relying on grants from the state of Tasmania, the city of Hobart, and—most likely—David's own gambling winnings.

Tasmania sounds quite exotic, but its name comes from the first European explorer who stepped onto this land, Abel Tasman. He named the island after his expedition's sponsor, Anthony Van Diemen, the governor of the Dutch East Indies. After the British seized the territory, they abandoned the Dutch name and, in 1856, christened the island after Abel Tasman—an effort to both honor the explorer and distance the island from the dark history of its penal settlements. Today, we call this rebranding! Tasman is also the name of a national park located in the Tasman Peninsula close to Hobart. Leaving its dark history behind and stepping into this national park, Tasmania reveals itself as a natural paradise, with nearly half of its land protected within national parks and World Heritage sites.

The environmental movement is strong under the stewardship of the Green political party—the world's first of its kind—dedicated to protecting Tasmania's unique ecosystem, home to plants dating back to the Cretaceous era. To protect this fragile environment, all potential sources of contamination must be kept at bay. Before entering any Tasmanian park, I had to clean my shoes—scrubbing the soles and applying disinfectant—to ensure I didn't bring in foreign soil or seeds that could disrupt the local species.

A wonderland of soaring sea cliffs and monumental rock formations, Tasman National Park is crisscrossed by trails porting hikers to impossible peaks, overlooking impressive chasms and white-sand beaches. The dolerite cliffs of Cape Hauy rise 300 meters from the depth of the ocean as if trying to cling to the white clouds above. These are Australia's tallest sea cliffs that run along the coast towards the other capes in the park. The hike to this spectacular cape is a test of endurance, ascending numerous steps carved into the hills with a total elevation gain of 600 meters. And I chose to climb them all on a hot summer day!

"From now on, I will always ride elevators instead of climbing steps in buildings. I had enough here..." said a Polish guy I met on the trail and with whom I hiked for a while.

When I reached the Cape Hauy overlook, I was suspended over an impossible chasm. More than a hundred meters down, the powerful ocean's waves seemed like tiny ripples, their force hinted at only by the white foam at their top. The surf hit the base of the Totem Pole, a 65-meter-tall sea stack so thin that I felt that at any moment it would break under its force. The treacherous Tasman Sea had pierced the rocks of the cliff, creating enormous arches or long, deep trenches as if a giant had swung an axe into the cliff, making a perfect cut. At the bottom of these trenches and in several other places along the shore, the waves' rhythmicity shaped Tessellated pavements, flat rock areas indented by perfectly straight lines, perpendicular to each other, drawn with geometric precision that did not seem to be just a whim of nature.

Tasman National Park is at the beginning of 'the nice road,' which stretches along the entire eastern coast of the island, and it's known by the tourist name of 'The Great Eastern Drive'. The next stop I discovered on this road was a stunning park, a place of wild beauty with a magic of its own. Freycinet is Tasmania's oldest national park, named after a French explorer who sailed through the area around 1800. Surrounded by the dramatic, towering pink-hued ridges of the Hazards, the powder-white beaches, and the transparent blue waters, Freycinet is the most photographed national park on the island. In any conversation in Tasmania, when I mentioned that I visited the national parks, the first question was if I had been to Freycinet. Wineglass Bay, a jewel in Freycinet National Park, serves as the centerpiece of one of the most captivating hikes in Tasmania. The 10-mile trail loops through the rugged terrain, climbing to an iconic overlook that offers a panoramic view of the bay's crescent-shaped shoreline. This breathtaking vantage point reveals Wineglass Bay in all its glory—a pristine arc of powdery white sand hugged by azure waters and framed by the dramatic granite peaks of the Hazards. It's a view so stunning and timeless that it has become synonymous with Tasmania itself, the crown jewel of its coastal landscapes.

WINEGLASS BAY, TASMANIA

For most travelers, the allure of Wineglass Bay doesn't end at the overlook. I felt its mesmerizing crescent curve attracting me like a magnet, inviting me to descend and immerse myself in its tranquil beauty. Even if I had no plans to walk along its shore, the hypnotic pull of the golden beach was irresistible. The feel of soft, powder-like sand underfoot and the soothing rhythm of crystal-clear waves brushing the shoreline created a meditative experience. Without realizing it, I found myself tracing barefoot the entire arc of the beach, lost in a reverie, each step carrying me closer to the soul of this unspoiled paradise. From the magical beach, a short trek through the forest brought me to another marvel: the Hazards' beaches. Here, the landscape shifts dramatically, with sheltered coves of striking red granite rocks. These formations created a stunning contrast to the turquoise waters that gently pooled in their embrace. The beaches of the Hazards, quieter and more secluded, offered a serene complement to the grandeur of Wineglass Bay. Together, these two bays—separated by a narrow strip of land—form a dynamic duality, showcasing the wild, untouched beauty of Freycinet National Park, which makes you feel as though you've stepped into a living postcard. If that hike was not enough, a short walk on Cape Tourville's boardwalk around its lighthouse offers a different view of Wineglass Bay in the distance, surrounded by tall peaks.

On the opposite shore, red and orange rocks called Nuggets are the exclusive domain of the seabirds. A sign read that if you sail straight east, you will arrive exactly at the middle of New Zealand's South Island. With no intention of venturing further, I spent the rest of the day unwinding on the beaches of Honeymoon Bay, where I found myself basking in the sun, lost in a daydream, as the golden hues of a glorious sunset painted the sky and water in breathtaking harmony.

As you continue to drive north, 'that nice road' turns out to be not so spectacular in itself, which makes you realize, something you suspected all along, that it's not the road, this Great Eastern Drive, that counts, but the collection of the amazing parks lined up one after another on the spectacular eastern coast of Tasmania. Otherwise, the road is like any other road with occasional houses, industrial sheds, garages, gas stations, and some farms where, occasionally, you may peek through and see the ocean bleached by the blazing sun.

When I reached St Helens in the north of the island, the road ended up in an explosion of fire, the last rays of the sunset spreading a bright red glow over the lichen on the nearby boulders. The next morning, I rose with the sun, eager to witness again the mesmerizing spectacle that unfolded over the Bay of Fires—a symphony of colors unlike anything I had ever seen before. As the first rays of dawn kissed the earth, the vibrant red hues of the lichen-covered rocks came alive, glowing with an almost otherworldly intensity. The fiery tones contrasted brilliantly with the pristine white sands and the crystalline turquoise waters, creating a scene so breathtaking it felt as though nature itself had taken up a paintbrush. The gentle whispers of the morning breeze and the rhythmic sound of waves breaking against the shore only heightened the moment's serenity, leaving me utterly captivated. In that golden hour, the Bay of Fires revealed its magic, a harmonious blend of raw, untamed beauty and peaceful tranquility—a moment of unparalleled wonder that I felt privileged to behold. Spanning a majestic coastline of 50 kilometers, the Bay of Fires extends from the captivating shores of Binalong Bay in the south to the iconic Eddystone Point in the north.

On the way, you discover the hidden gems of the Bay of Fires' coast, from the serene shores of the Gardens to the picturesque landscapes of its beaches, inviting you to rest there for days, weeks, or maybe forever. I followed the coast and hiked along it, looking for shade in a forest whose trees scrambled over the red rocks, occasionally touching the sugar-white sands. Pristine blue waters lapped gently at the powder-sand beaches, their calm waves surging now and then over red-hued boulders glowing fiercely in the midday sun. Here, 'that nice road' ends, and I felt the Bay of Fires to be its perfect finish, an enchanting red landscape of awe and wonder. The rugged terrain, strewn with megaliths shaped by ancient forces, speaks of the earth's deep history, while the tranquil waters and soft sands provide a soothing counterpoint to the land's raw power. It's a place where nature's palette comes alive, and I felt for a moment immersed in its captivating charm and infinite splendor.

CHAPTER 7

Fighting Gravity

IT'S ALL GOOD WHEN YOU DRIVE ON THE EASTERN COAST of Tasmania. Distances are short, and every two hours you reach another great national park. But when you arrive in St Helens, the road takes a turn and begins going inland. Little by little, you move away from the coast and, bracing yourself for a long drive, you aim towards the island's center. The road passes parks with picturesque waterfalls inviting for short hikes where you are dwarfed by the largest ferns that you have ever seen, pretty towns where mountain bikers zip around you like bees flying around a hive, lavender fields where the explosive purple of the plants is mixed with the ochre of the surrounding dirt, old pubs, like the Drunken Pig, the oldest in Tasmania that I found packed by Harley bikers, and a tropical forest of myrtle trees, relics as old as Gondwana—the primeval southern continent that once bound together the lands of the southern hemisphere before the oceans tore them apart.

Taking my time to soak in the stunning scenery along the way, I spent the entire day winding through the road before finally arriving in the evening at the Cradle Mountain campground, hidden in a deep forest nestled within the breathtaking Cradle Mountain-Lake St Clair National Park. By a stroke of luck, I had been able the previous day to secure the last bunk bed in one of the cabins, with no other places to sleep in the entire area, waiting till the last moment to see if the weather held, in this whimsical and unpredictable environment shrouded most of the time in a thick veil of mist and persistent rain. But even in terrible weather, the journey to this iconic Tasmanian landmark felt like a pilgrimage into the heart of raw and untamed beauty.

I found the room occupied by a very energetic young German and a sleepy Thai. The German, assertive as usual, was an IT engineer for a self-driving mobility company in Stuttgart. "I cannot tell you anything about it because everything is secret", not that I even asked him what he was doing for a living. He told me he had spent several months training for the Cradle Mountain ascent, and a few months ago, had booked the top bunk, where he had spread out the content of his backpack. I don't know,—maybe it's me—but each time I meet a German traveler, it seems they always pontificate, offering unrequested advice. My new friend started to shower me with advice about the next day's hike, wondering if I was fit for such an endeavor and asking me to reconsider. He was so sure of himself that I dared not even mention that I had no plans to climb the mountain. Based on previous experience, I kept quiet about the fact that I hadn't booked a reservation until the day before, knowing that such a confession would seem sacrilegious to any of his fellow countrymen. For preparation, I'd hiked and biked a lot, but lately, my workouts had been reduced to strolling barefoot on Tasmania's East Coast beaches or climbing the occasional Manhattan walk-up.

Meanwhile, in the other bed, the Thai guy was dozing, jet-lagged. As I later understood, he came here only to take a look, "because I saw some pictures on Instagram and they looked cool," and he did not have any plans of hiking because "I have no boots with me, just sandals".

Cradle Mountain is Tasmania's most iconic and breath-taking natural wonder, its dolerite peak standing proudly in the heart of the Tasmanian Wilderness World Heritage Area. With its jagged, wind-sculpted crest piercing the sky, it rises from the untouched landscape, a striking contrast against the serenity below.

I woke up early the next morning, crossing paths with a sleepy possum on my way to the bathroom, and found myself on the first bus into the park that dropped me at Ronny Creek, one of the stops at the beginning of one of the trails to the mountain.

Trails always start flat and inviting, seemingly a walk in the park. Nice lakes, flat paths, and lots of boardwalks covered in wire netting that prevent slipping, but are built to protect the fragile environment from the trampling tourists' boots. And Cradle Mountain's hikes were no exception. The weather was impeccable, quite unusual for this part of Tasmania: warm, with blue skies and perfect visibility. The day before, I mulled over various hikes around Cradle Mountain, but I never contemplated climbing higher than Marion Lookout, a spectacular viewpoint overlooking two lakes, Dove and Crater.

The Cradle Mountain summit hike is rated as hard on all hiking sites, and at this point in my life, I felt that I had nothing to prove anymore by reaching it. I started hiking up towards the lookout point, holding onto chains bolted into the rock while enjoying the amazing views. But things evolve organically, and you never know what may happen down the road. A relaxed chat with some hikers inspired me to continue from Marion Lookout to the Flat Track, a trail unfurling right under the peaks with a further descent to the lakes. But once on Flat Track at the base of the Cradle Mountain summit, the path up the mountain was packed like a boulevard at rush hour. Everybody and their grandmothers were going to ascend the summit. I asked several hikers how long it might take to climb the peak, and the estimate varied between two and four hours. Quite a margin! It did not seem so bad, and the weather was perfect.

CRADLE MOUNTAIN, TASMANIA

"As long as I am here…What the heck, I may go back if I don't feel like it…" I thought and decided to join the crowds and go towards the summit. What few who started the ascent knew, myself included, was that the hike up the mountain was not a hike but a climb, and this became obvious after about half an hour. The well-maintained trail with built-in steps morphed into a path of small rocks. Soon, the small rocks became boulders, and further up, they morphed into huge slabs. At one point, all you could do was climb one slab at a time and jump to another on an almost vertical trail. At this point, lots of people lost the enthusiasm garnered at the base of the summit and, after taking a selfie with the mountain, turned around.

For me, climbing seems like meditation. It's a process where you empty your mind and your only thought is on the next grip. How stable is it? Can it hold? How about the next step on that indent in the rock? Would my foot slip? One grip, one step, another grip, another step. You move up gently, swiftly, in no rush, with no other thoughts bothering you. There's no fear at all; it's simply focus. I used to free-climb in the Romanian Carpathian; nothing technical, no ropes, climbing on vertical tracks that were considered easy. But as easy as these tracks were, any slip or failed grip could have sent you tumbling in the best-case scenario to a hospital bed, if not to death. Since then, I've fallen in love with climbing and bouldering, taking every opportunity I could to practice. And the more I climbed towards the peak, the more I liked it. But no matter how much I loved it, I did not expect to have to climb huge slabs continuously for ninety minutes.

The false peak atop the vertical climb opened onto a rugged basin, seemingly sculpted by battling giants who hurled massive slabs at each other, covering the entire area. Negotiating these slabs, I descended towards its base only to have to climb its opposite vertical walls towards a steep trail that seemed to be going toward the peak. Though I had imagined myself hanging from a jagged peak at the summit, my expectations were shattered when I arrived at a flat top strewn with boulders and slabs, crowded with young people eating sandwiches and posting selfies—apparently a task more important than the climb itself.

Cradle Mountain, standing at just 1,545 meters, was first climbed in 1937 by Henry Hellyer, and a large cylindrical monument now marks the summit to commemorate his achievement. I took a short rest and began my descent, only to bump into the young German, looking slightly less energetic than inside the cabin, together with the Thai guy who was climbing the mountain in sandals. Both looked puzzled to see me descending from the peak:

"When did you leave in the morning? I did not think that you'd climb," said the German.

"Neither did I. I had no intention, but things happened... Anyway, hurry up because you will miss the bus," I said, referring to the tight schedule of the shuttle bus inside the park, without which you had to hike on the road several more miles.

The descent was as challenging as the ascent, if not more. It took almost the same time as the ascent, and, with aching legs, I reached the summit's base on the Flat Track. The pleasant descent from the summit's base toward Marion Lookout concealed what I feared was the toughest part of the hike: a sudden drop to Dove Lake along a trail almost entirely lined with chains, an extremely steep path carved into razor-sharp rocks. But after eight miles in eight hours and a 900-meter elevation, I finally found myself slumbering on the bus bench that carried me back to the campground.

One of the most influential figures in Cradle Mountain's history was Gustav Weindorfer, an Austrian-born botanist, mountaineer, and conservationist who fell in love with the mountain's striking peaks and pristine wilderness. At the beginning of the 20th century, Gustav visited the area and started a passionate campaign to preserve the region's natural beauty. He built Waldheim Chalet, a rustic cabin that became a hub for early visitors and adventurers seeking to experience the remote wilderness. Other explorers and naturalists followed in Gustav's footsteps, each drawn to the area for its raw, untamed landscapes, its rich biodiversity of pencil pines and the Tasmanian devils, the endemic carnivorous marsupials—one of their sanctuaries was near the campground—, as well as the challenge of ascending Cradle Mountain.

The next day, to everyone's surprise, the weather held with blue skies and warm weather in a climate where the descending clouds rarely let you see the rock comb of the Cradle Mountain peak. I needed to pay homage and visit the cabin built by this charismatic Austrian explorer who inspired so many with his enthusiasm for the mountain. I wandered around Dove Lake amid forests of banksia and manuka, the blossoms of which produce the region's famed, flavorful honey. The trail climbed to Wombat Pool—though no wombats appeared—before continuing upward to its summit and then descending toward Crater Lake. Along the way, a few wombats finally made an appearance, drawing the attention and cameras of hikers on the boardwalks, who snapped photos like paparazzi chasing Hollywood celebrities.

After two days of perfect weather, Cradle Mountain returned to its old habits, and the clouds were low, veiling everything in a wet mist. It was time to leave the mountain, and I said goodbye to the German guy who, patronizingly, commended me again for the fact that I was able to climb the peak. The Thai guy was still asleep, exhausted from climbing in sandals, and having missed the last bus, they had to walk six miles back to the campground.

I, meanwhile, began driving south toward Mount Field, a national park of waterfalls and tarns—small alpine lakes suspended by Mother Nature close to the sky. The almost five-hour drive—it's long to get to Cradle Mountain, but it's also long to get out of it, no matter where you go—passed through Sheffield, a town whose buildings were covered in murals and where I met Pedro, a traveling lama and his charming Tasmanian handler who stopped for pictures and stories.

About an hour away from Sheffield is Tasmania's oldest national park. Mount Field National Park, known for its remarkable diversity, spans from temperate rainforest to alpine vegetation, showcasing a stunning variety of plants that evolve with the changing altitude. At lower altitudes, the dense foliage of the ancient forest conceals several waterfalls and a grove of swamp gum trees—known as the 'Tall Trees Walk'—which soar up to 100 meters, creating an awe-inspiring, cathedral-like atmosphere. These trees, along with the myrtle beech, lend the area a prehistoric feel, as they are the descendants of the ancient forests that once covered Gondwana. Moss and lichens carpet the forest floor, thriving in cool, damp conditions, while fungi of all shapes and colors add a vibrant, otherworldly touch to the environment.

I went for a hike on a trail at a higher altitude that I found enveloped in an atmospheric mist. The Tarn Shelf, the best hike in Tasmania's alpine landscape, passes a myriad collection of tarns—small alpine lakes offering a breathtaking walking experience—following a trail that meanders past them, either along boardwalks or over jagged rocks. Near each large tarn is an emergency hut because in this environment, bad weather can be quite menacing. Hiking right under the Rodway Range, many dead pencil pines and eucalypts came into view in a desolate landscape torched by a fire caused by lightning. I was amazed at the hellish landscape, wondering if those trees would ever be able to recover, when I heard from behind:

"I don't know if you noticed, but most of the flora species are unique and can be found only in Tasmania." It was an older couple, both with backpacks and hiking sticks, that I soon found out were biology professors at the University of Hobart, so we dived into a discussion about the plants and trees of the alpine shelf. "Some of them share ancestral ties to species found in South America and New Zealand and trace back their roots to Gondwana, part of the Paleotropical Kingdom over 50 million years ago. Some of the plants and trees originated back in the Cretaceous era, something that only Tasmania can offer", he continued his lecture.

"I was looking around the tarn shelf, and it seemed to me that most of the bushes are different from what we have in Europe or America at similar altitudes," I said to him, pointing around to the tarns. Cushion plants formed dense, moss-like mats to survive the cold winds and snow. These low-growing plants created intricate, almost surreal mosaics across the alpine soil. Here and there, alpine daisies and heath shrubs added bursts of color to the otherwise austere environment.

"It's so great that you noticed this. So many people have no interest, and they hike here, dismissing these bushes as mere weeds. Chances are you'd never see these plants anywhere else. Look…", and he took some leaves from a bush, rubbed them between his fingers, and gave them to me to smell. "Try these," he said, giving me several other leaves.

"They are all perfumed and smell differently," he continued. "Most are endemic to the island, and we do our best to keep at bay seeds or dirt from other parts of the world that might taint and modify this environment. Without us humans around, these plants were able to survive through ice ages and shifting continents."

And seeing my enthusiasm, "One more thing for you because you come from America. You saw those pencil trees on the way. They were charred by lightning, and unfortunately, they won't recover. But they are derived from your American sequoia of California…"

"So, you say that they are from the Sequoia family?" I asked.

"Not exactly. They were, but they split from them 125 million years ago. Not too long ago, in the scale of geological eras, but they still shared the same ancient legacy. Tasmania is a living museum of botanical history," as he concluded his specialty talk.

I turned by the Twilight Tarn and started my descent through a dry brook, a fairly rapid 300-meter elevation drop over one kilometer, hiking through a eucalyptus forest with groves of snow gums and mountain pepper, a small shrub with spicy, edible leaves and berries. Before I reached the parking lot, Tasmania wanted to show off one more time its diversity with an iconic pandani grove, a prehistoric palm tree, the tallest heath plant in the world. With its serrated leaves of up to one meter, it might have resembled a monster ready to attack, making me feel that I had stepped by accident into another realm.

My time in Tasmania was almost over. I had thought a week would be enough, with a few days in Australia to follow—but after twelve days, I found myself unwilling to leave. But I had to be in New Zealand for another two weeks of already planned hikes. With only one day remaining, I returned to Hobart for the night to catch the ferry the next morning to my final destination.

Bruny Island—consisting of two islands, North and South—is quite long. A slender strip of land links the two islands, crowned by a gentoo penguin rookery on a central hill, now a popular tourist spot. The penguins appear only after nightfall, leaving visitors with little more than selfies. On the southern tip rises the lighthouse, Australia's second-oldest, offering breathtaking views from its top. The day trip from Hobart gave me just enough time for one longer hike, and I went for the Fluted Cape Circuit that ascends gradually through a serene eucalyptus forest, with razor grass bushes scattered along the forest floor. The Fluted Capes, a series of six striking rock formations, offer breathtaking views of the ocean and the surrounding rugged cliffs, where sheer drops plunge dramatically into the vibrant blue waters below.

Bruny Island is touted as a place to encounter Australia's endemic animals, yet aside from a solitary rabbit, the only other beings I saw were tourist groups herded onto buses—a sight I hadn't encountered elsewhere in Tasmania. The island's proximity to Hobart makes it a target for tour groups.

I returned to Hobart in the evening for the morning flight to Sydney and further to Christchurch, New Zealand. People were walking relaxed on boardwalks, eating ice cream, and softly chatting. Hobart remained as hushed as on my arrival, as though an unseen acoustic foam had swallowed every sound. A red moon rose over the harbor, reflecting its bloody disk in the mirroring waters. Total silence!

CHAPTER 8

THE LAST REFUGE

THE BEACH STRETCHED OUT TO THE FAR ROCKS; WHITE sand caressed by ripples of an ocean that seemed subdued by an invisible force. The palm fronds were waving in a breeze that seemed to come from nowhere. It seemed that everything else was at a standstill, frozen somehow by a miraculous spell. Among the branches, the moon rose, displaying its silvery discus in full splendor, adding to the mystery of the moment. No rustling sound seemed to come from the moving fronds above or from the lazy waves of the ocean. Absolute silence.

And at once, a strident shriek! Then silence. And another one, more desperate this time. And again. And again. My dream was shattered. At my screen door was a *moa,* a feral rooster of Kaua'i that I had heard of but had never seen before. He was puffing out his chest and crowing with gusto, announcing that the sun was up and that my glorious silvery moon had been just a dream. How this island came to be overrun by these creatures, rousing everyone at the crack of dawn, is anyone's guess—but local lore claims they escaped during the 1982 hurricane and have multiplied wildly ever since. And as in Florida's Key West, the feral chickens and roosters are protected, so I could not throw a shoe at him to shoo him away and go back to sleep. When I woke up, the boardwalk was already alive with people walking, jogging, and even doing yoga. Maybe the same rooster woke them up.

Kaua'i is small and preserves the atmosphere of a secluded island. Its map shows only one road that almost surrounds the island. And it was this 'almost' that intrigued me. Why did they not complete the road? Forced by the incessant crowing of the moa and this annoying question, I decided to get out of bed and find out why the two ends of this road do not meet.

Everywhere you go in Hawai'i, there's an intangible sense that something is slightly out of place, as if there's a hidden rhythm beneath the pulse of daily life. You're surrounded by towering hotels and sprawling resorts, manicured golf courses and sleek gyms, and massive supermarkets stocked with imported goods. Impeccably paved roads wind through lush landscapes, their smooth surfaces lined with modern cars and glitzy pickup trucks. The infrastructure of a fast-paced world is everywhere, making it easy to forget that Hawaii's soul operates on a much older, quieter frequency. But despite the modern backdrop, the people themselves seem to carry a timeless essence. The locals move through this world as if they belong to both the present and the past, embodying a unique duality. They drive their new trucks, wear modern clothes, and navigate contemporary life, but you can sense that they carry within them stories and spirits, gods and ancestors, as real as the ocean breeze or the mountains framing the horizon. This world, though unseen, pulses beneath their calm and unhurried demeanor, lending a mystical depth to the everyday actions. In Hawai'i, this connection to a world of gods and spirits is not merely nostalgia or cultural memory; it's part of the essence of the islands. We sought to explore this hidden side of Hawaiian life, subtle and elusive amid the glaring trappings of modernity in an archipelago now dominated by the new gods of comfort.

We left Kapaa, the largest town on the island, full of hotels and resorts to dive, for a short while, into the land of Kū, the god of war and politics. Hawaiian lore says that Kū arrived from his heavenly world and landed in Lāna'i amidst a storm. Once there, he became the protector of the Hawai'i archipelago, with special care for the chieftains' families. His *heiau* in Poliahu used to overlook the valley, protecting the area in a strategic location with sweeping views over the Wailua River. With his fearsome looks, Kū inspired terror in enemies, his tall statue once dominating the valley. Sadly, only three of the original Kū statues have survived to the present day. In Poliahu, as elsewhere, Kū was worshipped exclusively in temples, with strict and demanding rituals. Believers sought his aid in fishing, hunting in deep forests, and sometimes in farming.

A *heiau* is a Hawaiian temple built on a tall rock structure usually dedicated to a god. Some of them were places for human sacrifices to appease the gods in obtaining victory in war or protection from possible invaders. Those sacrificed were prisoners of war or people who broke a kapu by committing forbidden acts. Some *heiau* were not associated with deities but were built to mark sacred sites, such as the nearby Holoholoku Heiau, the birthplace of Kaumuali'i, the last king of an independent Kaua'i. Trying to fend off the expansionist tendencies of Hawai'i island's king Kamehameha, he made a pact with the English for protection. Yet the pact could not save him, and he became a vassal ruler of his island within the newly formed Kingdom of Hawai'i. The Wailua River was a silent witness to all these events, its crystalline waters flowing through the verdant valley in front of the temples, ending at Wailua Falls, a double fall where, in old times, Hawaiian men used to jump eighty feet down into a shallow pool following a local ritual. According to legend, none of the men who attempted the jump at the waterfall survived.

Every place you go on the islands feels cloaked in legends, each location steeped in stories that shaped its very existence. The power of these myths and ancestral tales is so great that they appear to blur the modern world encroaching upon them. Waimea Canyon, on the western coast of Kaua'i, is a vast chasm in the earth, where green streaks thread through brown peaks that extend to the horizon. Named the Grand Canyon of the Pacific, this one-mile-wide, 3000-foot-deep chasm has in its center the tallest peak of the island. We hiked the canyon trail on a path lined with native koa trees, only to find ourselves after about two miles, by the cool waters of Waipao'o Falls, seemingly small if you are afraid to peek towards its next 800-foot fall hidden by the lush vegetation. But as with many other places in Kaua'i, the canyon carries its legend. It is Poe's land of spirits where the people's souls go after they die. Here, the demigod Hiku went deep into the canyon to pull out, by a string, the soul of his beloved princess Kawelu after her death.

Leaving the realm of legend behind, we climbed into our car and followed the 18-mile winding road to Pu'u O'Kila, where Kalalau Beach stretched far below. Along the famous Na Pali Coast, featured in the *Jurassic Park* movie, Kalalau Valley and its beach unfold beneath a striking landscape of folded hills tumbling straight into the sea. This coast has no road access and is reachable only by hiking, if you don't count the queasy offshore boat visits or the buzzing helicopter rides. These precipitous hills create the gap in the road we were searching for.

"This is the last frontier, dude. The last piece of land where people can hide from civilization and nobody can find them," blurted a guy with long hair wearing worn-out jeans and a ripped T-shirt who came out of nowhere.

The valley was encircled by fluted capes, which, according to legend, were local children turned to stone by the winds when they failed to return home. It's a landscape of dramatic green ridges and waterfalls tumbling down sheer cliffs, all shrouded in mist carried by trade winds, sheltering a small valley floor once cultivated by the few Hawaiians who lived there. For the locals, Kalalau was a place of deep reverence, a valley imbued with profound spiritual significance. But all those people are long gone, their place taken by adventurers and squatters who, following the famous Kalalau Trail, made the valley their home—the last refuge in the U.S. where they could escape the confines and demands of the civilized world.

"It's a very tough hike," continued the guy. "You have to climb up and down for 11 miles. Steep and treacherous, man. One wrong step, and you're gone. You dive straight into the world of spirits. They are all gathered down there," he said with a smile.

Having been a haven for hermits, renegades, and hippies, the valley's access was tightly controlled by rangers, who allowed only five daily permits, all reserved long ahead of time. They patrol the valley by helicopters, forcing the squatters to hide when they hear the chopper. The rangers may show up inside the valley, but without enough forces, the chances of evicting the intruders are slim.

"Some of these dudes were once squatters down in the valley. And now they want to kick us out..." his words trailing while he began walking down towards the forest.

Eager to find the trail's origin, we drove away from Kapaa in the opposite direction, passing through a tunnel of luxuriant greenery so tall that the road seemed more like a hidden jungle trail. The winding road was lined with fields of taro. On the way, we stopped at a string of paradisiacal beaches where we hiked through forests of thatch screw pine trees with their roots up in the air until we reached the deep blue sea waves pummeling the black lava rocks of the shore. Not far from there, we reached the end of the road at Ha'ena Beach, a generous stretch of sand dwarfed by the huge cliff towering over it. Maniniholo Cave, tucked within the cliff, is said by local legend to have been the home of the Menehune, a mythical dwarf people who once roamed Kaua'i before the Polynesians settled the islands. Manini-holo, their chief fisherman, dug this cave to catch the akua (evil spirits) who were stealing the fish he caught during the day. In an unexpected encounter with the Polynesian settlers who pursued them, the legend says that the Menehune escaped through the cave to Waimea Canyon. But no one has ever discovered a path inside the cave beyond the one leading to the beach.

Despite our efforts to reach the Kalalau Trail, rangers tightly controlled access, and the parking lot was full. With no permit and no parking space available, and not being too keen on becoming squatters, we gave up trying to sneak into the mysterious roadless Na Pali Valley and spent the rest of the day on the beautiful beach, diving into the blue ocean surf and dipping into the river that flows into it.

CHAPTER 9

MEMORIES

THE STORY OF THE HAWAIIAN KINGDOM AND ITS SAD ending flows through the rooms of Iolani Palace, the royal residence of the last kings. Built in 1879 in the American-Florentine style, the palace is located in downtown Honolulu on the island of Oahu. Distinct from the surrounding high-rises, the building was outfitted with all modern amenities, becoming the first in Hawaiʻi to use electric lighting, four years ahead of the White House.

The Menehune, the Hawaiʻi's dwarf people, said to live in deep forests and hidden valleys, might have been a mythological creation, but what is documented is that the Polynesians started to arrive in Hawaiʻi around the beginning of the second millennium. According to legend, they were led by Hawaiʻiloa, a chief who conducted the canoe exploration of the archipelago. They spread across the islands, establishing independent settlements governed by chiefs, some of whom were related. The integration of the islands into a unified kingdom was done by Kamehameha I, who ruled over the large island of Hawaiʻi. At birth, his mother hid him from the warring clans in the secluded Waipi'o Valley on the side of Kohala Volcano, considered the gateway to Lua-o-Milu, the Hawaiian underworld, whose entrance was hidden somewhere in the sand. After the death threats passed, the mother took the child out of hiding and renamed him Kamehameha—the lonely one.

At the end of the 18th century, Kamehameha began a conquering campaign. Armed with European weaponry, he debarked in Maui in 1790 and, after a fierce battle, defeated the Maui king's army and conquered the island. The Iao Valley State Monument, built on the site of the battle, is centered around the Kukaemeko Peak, also known as 'the Iao needle'. A symbol of Hawaii's independence and historical and cultural significance, the 'needle' has been a lookout point for the scouts spying on the enemy's movement.

From Maui, Kamehameha moved his forces to Oahu, again obtaining a resounding victory. This victory brought the island of Oahu under his rule, together with Lanaʻi and Molokaʻi. Kauaʻi was supposed to be next, but the reigning king, Kaumualiʻi, aware of his slim chances of survival, yielded and offered both Kauaʻi and Niʻihau to Kamehameha I, who incorporated them into what would become the Kingdom of Hawaiʻi.

The United States overthrew the Hawaiian Kingdom at the behest of businesses with substantial interests in sugar and cattle. American and British businessmen arrived in Hawaiʻi at the end of the 18th century and established large plantations cultivating labor-intensive crops for export. Short of labor, they began bringing in migrants, and the local population soon started to dwindle in relative size. The businessmen advocated the takeover of the islands from local control, and in 1887, after several tries, they forced the king to sign a new constitution, nicknamed 'the bayonet constitution', which took away native Hawaiian land rights and gave the vote to the foreign landowners. Several years later, the Americans sent troops to Hawai'i and arrested its last ruling queen, Lili'uokalani, putting an end to an independent kingdom. After several more years, the archipelago was made a U.S. territory, and in 1959, it became the last state to join the Union. Today, the statue of the last queen, Lili'uokalani, stands defiantly before Hawaii's legislature, a reminder that she was the rightful ruler of the Hawaiian people in a nation still ambivalent about the American takeover.

The American occupation banned the Hawaiian language and suppressed local traditions, forcibly replacing them with American culture. However, in 1978, Hawaiian was declared the official language of the state, making Hawai'i the only U.S. state with an official language other than English. Following this, a revival took place, and nowadays, all streets, schools, local institutions, parks, and coastal points are written in the local language, and Hawaiian local traditions and sacred spaces are treated with the desired respect.

More than anything else, the island of Oahu and Honolulu are about memory; memories of men, heroes, kings, and gods. At the USS Arizona Memorial, the 1102 sailors who died on the infamous day of the Pearl Harbor attack of December 7, 1941, are remembered. The memorial was built on top of the wreckage of the navy ship, which lies beneath the surface of the sea. Oil from the ship's hull occasionally still leaks to the surface; black drops of memory spill, known as 'the tears of the Arizona'.

Memories are preserved in the Bishop Museum, a spectacular museum of anthropology where the three realms of the Polynesian world occupy the three floors of the museum: Kai Akea—the world of the sea, Wao Kanaka—the world of the people, and Wao Lani—the land of gods and kings. They are overseen by a large statue of Kū, and another of the god Lono, the two main deities of the islands. The Kū statue is one of only three of the god's effigies that survived. Gods dwell in Wao Lani, a place of silence where gods' *mana* still reverberates. The Hawaiians consider this land to be still on earth, but somewhere at higher elevations where men come only to gather rocks or collect medicinal plants. But to walk in that rarefied spiritual atmosphere, man must offer prayers to this realm and its godly inhabitants, asking for permission.

I wondered if permission was needed to walk the museum floor among these gods. Hawaiian deities were woven into daily life, manifesting in nature, the land, and human traits, reflecting a profound respect for the interconnectedness of the world. Each god has its own season, a time when it appears and governs the surrounding nature. During that time, the other gods are dormant or chilling in the background. Summer is dominated by Kane, the God of life, male sperm, sunlight, and freshwater, celebrated during the Summer Solstice. Kū is the god of the spring equinox, and Lono is responsible for the fall equinox. Sleep is associated with Kanaloa, Kane's brother, representing darkness. Celebrated during the Winter Solstice, he rules over the underworld in the depths of the oceans with their salty water and fierce winds, lording over navigators and the creatures of the sea.

All these gods were not perceived as distant figures issuing judgments from afar, but as active, integrated forces woven into the fabric of Hawaiian life. Working in harmony with the people, these deities offered guidance and protection, inspiring gratitude and reverence among the Hawaiians. Despite the encroachment of modern life, their presence remains undiminished, symbolizing the resilience of Hawaiian spirituality and the deep respect for the land that sustains the people.

CHAPTER 10

Don't Feed the Hippies!

THE MOST BELOVED FIGURE IN HAWAIIAN LORE—AND one celebrated throughout Polynesia—is the demigod Maui, quite a character, a kind of trickster who bent every rule and outwitted his opponents in the service of humanity. He is at the heart of countless legends, including tales of how he brought fire to the people and created the Hawaiian Islands by pulling them from the ocean depths with his enchanted fishhook, aumakua. This story was so influential that even the Māori of New Zealand credit Maui with pulling their North and South Islands from the sea. Also, with some of his canoe's vines weaved together, he threw his magical hook towards the sky, lassoing the sun and stopping it in its celestial arch, making it shine longer during the day to help the humans. According to another legend, Maui lifted the sky, which had been too close to the earth, giving humans the room to stand tall. To help his own family, Maui fought the huge monster lizard Kuna, which tradition says lurks around ponds and waterfalls.

The lizard had blocked a river, flooding the cave where Maui's mother, the goddess Hina, lived. Maui rescued her and then turned the monster to stone near Rainbow Falls on the Big Island of Hawai'i. With such an impressive resume, it is no surprise that one of the Hawaiian Islands was named after him!

BAMBOO ON PIPIWAY TRAIL, MAUI

On Maui, a rock-stepped trail winds through a forest of dry trees before giving way to a mysterious tropical jungle crossed by a cascading river spanned by charming bridges. The idyllic Pipiwai Trail passes a series of more than seven pools and waterfalls, all draped in a lush green blanket that seems to belong to another world. A hole in this green blanket offers a peek towards a towering sheer cliff. Makahiku Falls plunges 200 feet over a cliff draped in bamboo and giant ferns, entwined with jungle vines, resembling a theatrical set for an exotic film. Surrounded by lush foliage that spilled like a green waterfall into the pool below, we felt as if we had stepped into a film set—a gigantic bathtub fit for Kū himself. And almost on cue, when we turned a corner, we came upon a massive banyan tree, its interwoven branches and trunks sprawling in all directions, each seeming to grow from another. A mesmerizing view that inspired the natives to consider this tree the symbol of eternal life.

And if this was not enough, the dramatic landscape soon changed into an explosion of emerald green sticks squeezing you from all sides; an encompassing bamboo forest looking super-zen made of large and small bamboo clumps, dead bamboo, and fallen bamboo, but most of all, majestic trunks that you can barely encircle with the fingers of two hands. The stepped trail unfolded somehow apologetically under a canopy of dignified bamboo that crisscrossed above our heads like spears in a fight among the invisible but for sure present spirits of the forest. The javelins' dueling reverberated in the hollow percussive sounds created by the bamboo stalks striking one another, an ambiance that might transport you to an Asian netherworld. The tops of these bamboo spears have green leaves that sway in the breeze. The forest is thick and hard to enter, but if you can find a spot to squeeze into it, a look from below makes these bamboo stems look like veins reaching for the gods who sip through them an invisible elixir from the enchanted pools. The bamboo trail snakes over the rugged, scarred earth, finally arriving at the foot of the breathtaking 400-foot Waimoku Falls. This is He wai makamaka 'ole, 'the water that recognizes no friend.' Waimoku means water that cuts, severs, amputates, and breaks things in two, as often happens after heavy rains. From afar, the mountain reveals not one but four waterfalls of varying heights, all crashing into a tumultuous river that winds through Oheo Gulch toward a turbulent ocean dotted with black lava.

Pipiwai Trail and Oheo Gulch lie within Haleakalā National Park on Maui, a compact park accessible from Kihei via a rough, one-lane, rugged coastal road that hugs the cliffs with nothing but the abyss below. On one side of the one-lane road are sheer cliffs, and on the other side, straight down, the blue of the ocean. Nearby Haleakala, 'the house of the sun', invites you to the great show of the sunset. The winding road climbing the volcano is peppered with signs asking drivers to beware of the slow-moving Hawaiian goose Néné, parading in the Hawaiian spirit. Néné are endangered, and a lot of attention is paid to the bird and its food, a specific berry bush growing in the desert fields.

The dormant Haleakala volcano, on whose peak the demigod Maui famously seized the sun, rises over the island of Maui, visible from almost anywhere. Its crater, a Mars red landscape of cones dressed in ashes of various colors, is a demonstration of nature's power in every sense. At the bottom of the huge caldera is a collection of cinder cones, lava flows, and dikes formed when magma cooled, all flecked by pieces of magma once collected by the Hawaiians to make sharp tools.

The Sliding Sand Trail (Keonehe'ehe'e) descends into the crater on a path that you can see from the top, almost all of it winding through a sea of volcanic ash that cracks under trampling boots. The hike itself isn't difficult, but the 10,000-foot altitude tests your lungs and stamina. Inside the crater, the red cones, bathed in the slanting orange rays of the weary sun, beckon us to continue exploring. From the rim, one side of the volcano disappears into clouds and dampness, while the other remains clear and dry. At 10,023 feet, Haleakalā's summit holds the clouds at bay—a striking example of atmospheric inversion. Unsurprisingly, the peak is dotted with telescopes watching the sun, while the moon and other celestial objects are monitored by a large astronomical complex operated by the U.S. Department of Defense. Tourists flock to the peak, some at sunrise, but mostly at sunset, to admire the sun setting in its own house.

HALEAKALA VOLCANO, MAUI

Descending Haleakala, we left behind the demigod Maui and Pele, 'the goddess who dug the fire pits', and we continued around the edge of the volcano's caldera until we reached the most famous road in Maui. Hana Road is also named Hana Highway, which seems a misnomer for a road that, in large part, has only one lane! Its 64 miles is an exercise in driving endurance. The narrow road twists along the coast and winds into the island's interior, occasionally opening onto dramatic bays where jagged volcanic rocks keep visitors from the shore, despite the inviting palm trees that shade a nonexistent beach. No sand—only black, sharp, unwelcoming rocks. Occasionally, a small black sand beach is the best the volcanic environment can offer.

Waterfalls and small brooks caress the surrounding cliffs, gushing from the depths of the forest towards the road, passing under the one-lane bridges to the ocean; a forest full of gigantic ferns and the rainbow eucalyptus, a palette of hues over the blanket of surrounding green. Small one-lane bridges force traffic to a halt, and there are so many of them, letting the incoming traffic pass while people get out of their cars to take pictures. Occasionally, clumps of parked cars flag the start of a hiking trail to waterfalls hidden in the tropical forest. The Twin Falls trail, located on a private farm, was lined with tropical plants. The short hike ended at an ablution pool that seemed made for the forest's gods. It is fed by two almost Siamese falls plunging from a tall cliff, soaking the heated bodies and souls of the less godly tourists who were chilling under the incessant flow as if in a cleansing ritual. More waterfalls appear on the other side of the road. Waimea Falls is small, but nearby Wailua Falls plunges apparently from the sky, surrounded by a forest that seems to crawl up the sheer cliff. Water goes down, plants go up. The road is packed with tourists that seem to be the only humans around, but finally, in the Hana Peninsula, we see locals hauling a wild boar in the back of a pick-up truck. The hunt of the day, an old tradition, and an environmental control of the feral pigs that damage crops.

The drive through the tropical forest was exciting but also very long, and with so many traffic stops and lookout points, it took us an entire day and ended in the tiny town of Paya, populated by hippies, all gathered in a parking place with their tents and supermarket carriages where they keep their belongings.

A sign at the town's entrance reads emphatically: 'Do not feed the hippies.' Around Paya, the deep forest disappears, replaced by fields and farms descending towards beaches where locals surf, far from the menacing, sharp lava rocks along the shore, near bays where giant tortoises swim.

The landscape change brought a switch in the gods' realms. The land of Kū gave way to the realm of Lono, two facets of life that highlight its inherent duality and contrasts—from the austere domain of Kū, god of the chiefs, to the more relaxed realm of Lono, god of the people. In ancient Hawai'i, Lono was believed to have come from a distant land, first arriving in Maui, bringing with him agriculture, growth, germinating plants, and fertility. All these, together with the rain and storms, and the animals that dug the ground like pigs, were considered manifestations of Lono. He dominated local life for about four months until the fall equinox, when the crops were gathered. During this time, peace prevailed because everyone needed crops to survive, so Lono was also known as the god of peace. Lono was honored in grand festivals such as Makahiki, held a thousand years ago in Iao Valley in front of Kūkaemoku Peak—the stone phallus of Kanaloa, god of darkness and the ocean. There, the Hawaiians gathered to honor the god through hula, the dance invented by Lono's wife, Laka. When Lono's staff effigy was paraded through the fields, Kū's temples were closed. Both gods could not be in the same place at the same time. Kū was worshiped only in temples that had huge statues, while Lono could be worshiped anywhere across the islands. Neither the Kū statues nor the Lono staff were considered gods by the Hawaiians, but just effigies that the gods were invited to occupy following a set of specific rituals and prayers. Partnering with the male gods were the vahine, female gods, in charge of similar chores as the gods but sometimes in different locations or taking care of specific tasks, like childbirth or keeling.

We watched surfers dance on the never-ending waves till sunset. Boys and girls tried to stand on water, waiting patiently to catch a tall wave, which would make them glide on their flimsy boards. Perhaps they were children of gods who once rode these waters, some gliding atop towering waves all the way to the moon, to join the goddess Hina and find shelter in her luminous silvery disc.

CHAPTER 11

The Volcano's Fiery Diva

THE WIND WAS BLOWING WILDLY IN THE DARKNESS, and rain was pelting the windows, making them shake. The van didn't arrive at 5 a.m. to pick us up, and no message came to inform us that our morning ascent of Mauna Kea, the Big Island's highest peak, had been canceled. We huddled back in bed and checked the mail, only to realize that the Internet was down.

"What do you expect? We are on an island! Be happy when we have it…", our host said, unfazed when we asked how long we would be without the Internet, a real first-world tragedy.

According to tradition, the Mauna Kea volcano, also known as the White Mountain, was created by the gods. All other volcanoes were shaped by nature. The White Mountain carries the name of Wakea, the sky father who, by marrying Papahanaumoku, the Earth Mother, gave birth to the local chieftains of the Hawaiian Islands. According to legend, White

Mountain is the place where life began in the archipelago. It is believed to connect the realm of the gods with the underworld, serving as a place of spiritual power, bridging the two worlds. Its slopes are dotted with altars and sacred burial grounds. In ancient times, only the *kahuna* (priests) were allowed to visit the summit. All others were forbidden, bringing a death sentence upon the trespasser. For us, Mauna Kea's peak was also unreachable. Snow and fog veiled the mountain, and its summit was closed for days in a row. All the trips from Hilo to the peak were canceled, and money was returned to the credit cards.

Mauna Kea, the tallest peak in the Pacific, rises 13,679 feet above sea level, but when including its 19,700 feet hidden below the ocean, it is the tallest mountain on Earth, surpassing even Mount Everest. According to legend, the goddess Pele made Mauna Kea her temporary home in Hawai'i. Today, her abode is protected by National Park Service rangers, who forbid anyone without a proper 4×4 and a permit from driving to the summit and disturbing the goddess.

Just across the Mauna Kea access road lies a route that leads all the way to the Mauna Loa Solar Observatory, towering at over 11,000 feet. Mauna Loa is the largest active volcano in the world. In 2022, it erupted simultaneously with Kilauea, creating a spectacular display that drew crowds to Hawaii's Big Island. The well-maintained one-lane road winds through a sea of roped lava fields, reaching its end right in front of the observatory gate. From there, an eight-hour trail climbs another 3,000 feet to the mountain's peak.

No god is more revered in the archipelago than the goddess Pele, whose abode seems to be in Kilauea volcano on the island of Hawai'i. According to legend, Pele was born in Honuamoa in Tahiti. She descends from Haumea, the primordial Earth goddess, and Kane Milohai, architect of the sky, earth, and the upper heavens. Pele's mythology counts no more than 16 sisters, 13 of whom are named Hiiaka. Was this a trendy name among the gods or a lack of parents' imagination?

Her passionate character led Pele to seduce her brother-in-law, raising the wrath of her sister Namakaokahai. In addition, the hot-tempered goddess-to-be of volcanoes, fire, lightning, and dance,—a passionate and beautiful woman—fell in love with mortal men as well as gods and, in a fit of rage or jealousy, according to legend, turned them into dogs or trees or banished them to uninhabitable parts of the islands. Her fiery temper led her father to send her away from home. She found her way to Kaua'i but ended up being discovered and chased by her sister, who viciously attacked her and left her for dead. Somehow, Pele was able to recover and escaped to Oahu, where she started to dig fire pits, including Diamond Head, the largest crater on the island. She pursued her new hobby across several islands, finally reaching Maui, where legend has it she dug out the Haleakala volcano. Finding out that Pele survived, Namakaokahai traveled to Maui, and in an epic battle near Hana, she tore her sister apart. Through her death, Pele became a goddess, making her lair on Mauna Kea on the island of Hawai'i. There she dug her final fire pit, the Halemaumau Crater at the summit of Kilauea, which people consider to be her abode.

Pele is also the goddess of creation and destruction and is known as 'the woman who devours the land.' Hawaii's volcanic eruptions are all attributed to her. From her crater's abode, she manifests her anger by whimsically sending lava down the mountain, dramatically changing the landscape and shaping the islands. Honoring Pele and praying to her is a long-standing tradition, observed by both everyday people and royalty alike, seeking protection for their homes against eruptions. According to legend, King Kamehameha cut his hair—considered the repository of his *mana* in Hawaiian tradition—and offered it to the volcano, pleading with Pele to halt an eruption. In Mauna Loa, Pele is said to have sent a white dog to warn her family of impending lava flows, a tale so enduring that even in the 1950s, people reported seeing a white dog roaming the slopes, disappearing and reappearing years later. Local folklore also tells of Pele manifesting on modern roads as an old woman with white hair, hitching rides with unsuspecting drivers before vanishing when they turn to look. Perhaps she even rode with us, though we didn't dare look back to see.

We tried to find traces of Pele in Kilauea, part of the Volcano National Park, where signs of recent eruptions, fields of lava, and numerous craters dotted the side of the road crossing the park. Kilauea Iki Trail skirts the Iki crater on one side and continues towards the bottom. The path to the crater cuts through a dense forest before emerging onto a vast expanse of hardened lava, encircled by hills of ash and jagged rocks. The trail follows the crater's rim from where we could see smoke rising from the nearby active Halemaumau pit. It further descends inside the caldera following a line of ahu, stacked rocks in a desolate landscape of lava slabs covered in moss and pierced occasionally by timid flowers and saplings.

The bottom of the crater was a flat sea of magma collapsing on itself. It seemed as if a giant worm had traveled under it and displaced huge meter-thick lava slabs that were flipped and broken by the force of the movement like flimsy pieces of cardboard. Some magma looked like ocean waves frozen in their hideous movement, confusing even the gods. The ahu helped us navigate the immense crater, bringing us to the opposite side, back into a forest alive with flowers and ferns, stretching eagerly toward the sky above the surrounding trees. From desolation to a vibrant life once destroyed by an incandescent flow.

The 1959 volcanic explosion, which reached 580 meters—higher than the world's tallest buildings—lasted 37 days and left hills layered with ash, resembling mountains formed over geological eras. We squeezed into a lava tube, a long tunnel created by the once-molten lava. When the lava flow stopped, the hot magma inside continued to pour downhill, leaving a tunnel behind where you can walk upright through the cavernous interior lit by spotlights mounted on the sides.

Invited or not by Pele, we went for a hike toward her home in Halemaumau Crater on a trail shaded by the most gigantic ferns we had ever encountered. The land was fractured, with steam vents that seemed like gateways to a boiling netherworld beneath. Along the boundary fault encircling Kīlauea, Keanakāko'i Crater lay blanketed in lava and cinders, draped with ash, its floor resembling a waterless lake shrouded beneath a smooth expanse of dark magma. This crater once provided the hard rock Hawaiians used to craft adze, their sharp axe. From the rim, the view towards the Kilauea caldera is of a boiling inferno. A gigantic hole in the ground expands as far as you can see, where smoke rises from the boiling molten lava that pours onto the surface, the orange of the eruption partially concealed by the blazing sun. Here, the land shifts daily. Photos on display reveal how the caldera expanded over the last decade. Thousands of earthquakes rocked the region, culminating in the 2018 collapse of the rim that engulfed the Jaggar Museum and the Hawaiian Volcano Observatory.

The road snaked through Volcanoes National Park, flanked on both sides by coiling, intertwined lava ropes that seemed frozen in mid-motion. From Mauna Ulu, a fissure travels for five miles in a desolate landscape. The petrified lava leaves behind fantastic shapes, creatures of a frozen inferno, and ghosts arrested in the landscape.

In this bleak environment, Hawaiians were able to find hope and rebirth. Pu'u Loa (Long Hill) is the largest petroglyph field in all of Polynesia. For generations, Hawaiian families came, and still come today, to Pu'u Loa to place the umbilical cord (*piko*) of their newborn in small holes (*puka*) they dig in the field's volcanic rock, hoping for a long life for their children. The tradition says that the field's *mana* will bless their child and connect him to the ancestral land. Some *puka* are large and deep; others are shallow, depending on who dug them. Amid the scattered holes, the volcanic rocks are inscribed with figures and symbols, echoes of a civilization without a written language. Comparable anthropomorphic carvings can be found at the Puakō Petroglyph Preserve on the western coast, which contains roughly 1,200 petroglyphs in the public area and many more in the surrounding landscape, portraying humans, gods, and animals. The same representations are found at Waikoloa Field, now encircled by golf courses and resort villas—a stark contrast between civilizations. Yet, for the Hawaiians, these places once held deep significance, where they gathered for important moments in their lives or to honor their gods.

PETROGLYPHS, HAWAI'I

The road ends at the southern tip of Hawai'i Island, Ka Lae, a holy site for the locals. The perfectly squared Kalalea Heiau was an ancient fishing shrine dedicated to Ku'ula, the god of fishing. It is still visited today by fishermen who bring offerings, thanking the god and hoping for a good catch. On the nearby stone-paved platform, the fishermen prepared the fish for meals or sacrifices. The salt left behind after seawater evaporated, collected in nearby carved rectangular pans, was used to preserve fish. Scattered around the *heiau* are sacred stones honoring the male and female aspects of Kanaloa, the god of the ocean: a navigation stone, one for meditation before dangerous fishing trips, and a large table stone thought to have served the chiefs' (*ali'i's*) wives during childbirth. Another birthing stone, the Hauola Stone in Lahaina, Maui, has been used by *ali'i's* wives since the 14th century and continues to serve as a healing site.

The Chain of the Craters Road ends here in this mythical place where beliefs never die. It's also the most southern point of the USA, something that divides more than unites these two cultures. Surrounded by all these stones, some sculpted by Hawaiians hundreds of years ago, I sat on the cliff overlooking the shore contemplating Holei Sea Arch through which a spectacular sun was inching its way to the other side of the world.

Surprisingly, after dark, traffic in Volcano National Park increases, and local families and tourists come in procession with grandparents and small kids in tow to visit Pele's home by night. Crowds line the road to the burning Halemaumau crater, yet all that meets the eye is a parade of phone lights flickering through the darkness. They all moved as in a religious procession that reminded me of Easter midnight in Eastern Europe. And Pele is at home, fiery and passionate, in full swing, throwing a tantrum of molten lava into the air and coloring the night sky in red velvet.

The restaurant terraces filled with sunhats and sunglasses, cocktails in hand; golf courses, high-end shops, beaches lined with umbrellas and lounge chairs, and boats drifting leisurely along the shore, present a picture of a paradise catering to the world's desires. Watching the locals, one sees their reverence for ancestral traditions, their gentle humility, and enduring spirituality—a living testament that the islands are far more than a mere tourist destination. Hawai'i is a place steeped in mythology, where legends linger and spirits watch over the land. Hawaiians do not consider the legends about gods and heroes as myths. They understand them as historical facts, and their recollection represents the knowledge by which they conduct their social and spiritual lives. Many of the legends in Hawai'i, like the ones found in New Zealand, describe the sacred genealogy of the people of the archipelago. Their connection with their ancestors is also achieved through the traditional *hula* dance, which is a form of meditation. *Hula* is believed to come from the gods, and Laka, Lono's wife, is credited with transmitting this knowledge to the people. Tradition speaks of the connection between dancers and audience, through which the power of *mana* is transmitted, with the dancers conveying knowledge via oral storytelling.

There are no fewer than 44,444 gods named *akua* that rule the lives of the people of Hawai'i, each *akua* with its specific power and rank. The manifestations of *akua* are also represented in the *ki'i*, the tangible images of these deities. They also take earthly forms, known as *kinolau*, manifesting as natural phenomena, plants, or animals—each with a role to play in the world inhabited by the Hawaiians. The *akua* also include the *aumakua*, ancestral spirits worshiped by families, manifested in creatures of the sea, such as sharks and octopuses, as well as in owls, lizards, and other animals. These guardian spirits, long central to Hawaiian family traditions, are believed to possess magical powers. An *aumakua* might appear as a bird perched on a branch or a sea turtle in a nearby pond—signs to be interpreted but always respected, lest misfortune follow. Among Hawaiian superstitions are the night marchers: spirits of ancient warriors who, having once patrolled vast battlefields, are believed to wander the islands by night, chanting and bearing torches. They appear as ghostly apparitions, some playing drums, who might kill you if you look them straight in the eye. Superstitions also caution against whistling or cutting plants at night, as doing so might summon harmful spirits.

The system of religious, political, and social laws that ruled Hawaiian society for centuries was known as *Aikapu*. Conceived by the priests, it permeated all of Hawaiian life, shaping political decisions, war strategies, sacred ceremonies, and everyday events such as births and the planting of crops. With so many gods to respect, traditional Hawaiian society had strict rules. Known as *kapu*, the intricate code of laws was meant to protect religion and assure a safe lifestyle for the inhabitants of the islands. *Kapu* also meant a sacred interdiction, a law so strict that even the slightest trespass could bring a death sentence. *Kapu* also mandated what people could eat, where they could go, and how they were supposed to behave in certain situations in society. Among the *kapu* rules were bans on men and women eating together, restrictions that barred women from certain foods, and the eerie prohibition against touching another person's shadow or reflection. The strict enforcement carried out by a *kapu* keeper was necessary because it was believed that a person who committed a grave sin was threatening the spiritual power of the society by stealing *mana*, the spiritual energy of the group. And everything revolved around *mana*, which conferred sacred power as the life force within all things. With so many laws and interdictions that varied from one season to another, it was no wonder that many inhabitants were threatened with execution. For those incriminated, the Hawaiians developed refuge places. Pu'uhonua O'Honaunau on the Big Island was such a place. The condemned had to escape—often by swimming—to reach this sanctuary, where a local priest could offer pardon, letting them dwell untouched by the vengeance of society.

The *Aikapu* system lasted until the death of Kamehameha I, and the system's demise, brought on by his successors, fundamentally changed Hawaiian society. It was the 1819 Battle of Kuamo'o that finally defeated the last supporters of the *Aikapu* system. Their defeat brought the destruction of the *akua* and the *ki'i* of the gods across the island, like the ones for Kū. The new constitutional monarchy envisioned a more egalitarian society, restricting chiefs from abusing or overtaxing their subjects. At the same time, the monarchs began to regard education and healthcare as fundamental pillars of society, maintaining an almost universal level of literacy. However, the world was changing rapidly, with American business interests quietly maneuvering behind the scenes. In the following years, Hawaiian society unraveled, and its culture was obliterated. The rhythms of *hula* were overtaken by rock and roll, and the gods once revered faded as American politicians took their place.

Yet the profound and spiritual essence of the islands endured, and the core values of Hawaiian spirituality persisted. Even with the ancient gods gone, the reverence for ancestors and respect for the unseen world remained a vibrant part of the Hawaiian identity. The Hawaiian Islands embody a living spirit. Rooted in *aloha,* their way of living is imbued with love, and *'āina,* a deep respect for the environment perceived not as a resource to exploit, but as a family member to care for. Its spirit reflects a harmony between the land, the ocean, and its people. It flows through the waves that lap against ancient shores, the winds that carry ancestral stories, and the songs that are sung beneath starlit skies. Through every transformation, the essence of *aloha* endures, reminding everybody that the true heart of Hawai'i cannot be erased, only shared.

CHAPTER 12

Kia Ora to the New Gods

ANYWHERE IN THE WORLD, LANDING IN AN AIRPORT brings you the déjà vu: a slick new building, long lines for passport controls, taxis lined up at the curb, other slick buildings along the road, crowds of people, traffic, fumes. Boring! But when the legends begin to weave like in a cocoon, what we call modernity somehow starts to feel different. You still find yourself in a modern technological city made of glass and steel, rebuilt after an earthquake caused by the stirring of a giant, buried by a legendary folk hero, under a heap of earth in a nearby peninsula. That legendary folk hero is credited with many other feats, like pulling islands out of the ocean, lifting the sky, or slowing the sun. Upon such fertile ground for ancestral legends, new storytellers—weavers of modern myths of dancing images—planted their own mystical tales, filled with fantastic beings in search of powerful amulets. These new legends came to life in our lifetime, breathing magic into a land that seems to belong to gods and heroes—rather than humans—and which we, the *Pākehā*, call New Zealand. *Kia Ora*!

"You know that English is not the official language of New Zealand," my friend told me when I said that I might go there.

What did he mean? Every Kiwi I encountered, as the locals are affectionately known, spoke English. Yes, with that funny accent that required me to ask them twice what they wanted to say. Different from the Aussies' accent, the Kiwis seem less assertive in a way, but you can find them roaming in many parts of the world.

"We take a year off after we finish college and travel the world," a Kiwi once told me. "We are so far away from everything that once we leave, we try to see as much as we can".

I could never have imagined that they spoke a language which, though not the official one, is still spoken by nearly the entire population and is even used by the government. I began reading to uncover a culture that, until then, had been hidden by our ignorance, folded into the vast distance separating us from these remote Pacific islands.

In the Pacific, legends feel woven into contemporary life. They are retold casually as current events by relaxed locals gathered around a drink on the beach. You don't even know if what they said actually happened or if somebody just made it up, yet the tales remain remarkably exact and oddly familiar, even in their otherworldliness. Delving into this cultural chasm, I stumbled upon the story of the Māori people, whose oral tradition claims their origin in a magical place named Hawaiki. Where exactly this place is, nobody knows, even though many have gone on voyages in search of it. But Hawaiki refused to surrender its secrets, shrouding itself in the enigmatic aura of mythology. Historians often associate it with Tahiti, despite its name echoing the distant Hawaiian Islands. In Māori tradition, however, Hawaiki holds a sacred place: the realm from which Io, the supreme being, shaped the world and breathed life into its first inhabitants. It is also the ultimate destination of each soul after death.

"Our souls travel to Hawaiki after we die," said one Māori man I encountered later in Rotorua. With his dark skin and elaborate tattoos, he looked as if he had stepped out of legend, yet there he was, leaning against a silvery Ford pickup, tapping away on his iPhone.

In any case, it is a known fact that the Māori sailed the Pacific to New Zealand, a land that in their oral tradition is called Aotearoa, 'long cloud'. They embarked on these voyages somewhere between 1250 and 1350 in two migration waves. It is still debatable where they were coming from. The anthropologists point towards the Polynesian islands, a sort of hub from where the Pacific population spread towards the surrounding islands. But if you go back in time, the mystery thickens because these ancestors' lineage can be traced back almost 5,000 years to the indigenous peoples of the island we know today as Taiwan. The migration began in the second millennium BC. From there, in the next two millennia, taking advantage of anomalous cyclones, Polynesian people dispersed across a vast area of the Pacific. They journeyed across Tonga, Samoa, Tahiti, Hawai'i, the Chatham Islands, Pitcairn, and Easter Island (Rapa Nui), and, of course, New Zealand, lands scattered across a vast ocean yet bound together by dialects still remarkably similar today. In New Zealand, they first settled on the northern island in the second part of the 13th century and finally secured a more permanent settlement after the Tarawera Volcano eruption of 1315.

They lived and wove their stories. Stories about gods descending from the sky and becoming mountains, gods of the forests who made light by separating the earth and the sky, and stories about mythological creatures living on high peaks. They fought among themselves, forging tales of courage and valor in their conquests, until October 1769, when the arrival of Captain Cook and the HMS Endeavour forever changed the lives of these local tribes. The incessant encroachment of the English onto their territory made the tribes put their swords aside, and 80 years later, on February 6, 1840, representatives of the British Crown and Māori chiefs signed the now-famous Treaty of Waitangi. The agreement aimed to establish a partnership that would ensure the protection of Māori rights while facilitating British colonization. Māori chiefs affirmed their sovereignty, demanding equal rights as British subjects while asserting their ownership of lands, forests, fisheries, and all other treasured possessions. However, as usual, things get lost in translation, and the Englishmen wrote in their transcribed version that the Māori Chiefs ceded the sovereignty of their territories.

At Te Papa, the Museum of New Zealand in Wellington, we came upon the Treaty's articles, presented in Māori and English, etched into two towering wooden panels that face each other across the museum's main hall, as if in an eternal dialogue. While the Māori language version was visually clear, many parts of the English version were covered in spray paint following a large protest that saw one of the protesters abseil from the museum ceiling and deface the panel that stated the ceded sovereignty. That mistranslation opened the door to sweeping land confiscations, systemic abuses, and deep grievances that still reverberate today. And this simple, but probably not unintentional mistake, took more than a century to be addressed. In 1975, the Waitangi Tribunal secured a settlement with the Crown regarding the land confiscations after the 1840s. It was a remarkable victory for the Māori. The agreement also included a formal apology from the Crown, symbolizing acknowledgment of past wrongs. In the decades that followed, the Māori gradually brought their culture into the mainstream. Their language, once discouraged and even ridiculed, was later recognized as an official language of New Zealand, alongside the Māori sign language. Nowadays, English is the de facto language, the government language, a sort of lingua franca, but NOT the official language of New Zealand. Today, Māori is a mandatory subject in schools, and even if children don't become fluent, they still grow up able to understand their Māori friends. About 17% of New Zealand's population identifies as Māori, while roughly 71% identify as Pākehā, or European New Zealanders. Yet, given the high rate of intermarriage, it is estimated that nearly a quarter of the population has Māori heritage. It was a captivating story, one that left me mesmerized.

Everywhere I traveled in the Pacific, I witnessed a revival of traditional cultures, resilient enough to withstand the tide of uniformity that so often accompanies modern development. Yet, nowhere did I feel the local pride as strongly as in New Zealand, where the success of the Māori in preserving their heritage and resisting complete colonial assimilation stands as a powerful testament to their resilience and identity. But let's start weaving the stories of the Māori by walking on their land.

CHAPTER 13

In the Magical Worlds of Lewis and Tolkien

THE ENIGMATIC REALM OF KURA TAWHITI—BETTER known as Castle Hill—rises between the east and west coasts of Te Waipounamu, New Zealand's South Island. Its other-worldly terrain of limestone boulders, sculpted by time and nature into gigantic shapes, is reminiscent of ancient castles trampled by history. To the Māori tribe of Ngai Tahu, the largest tribe of the southern island, this place holds profound historical, spiritual, and cultural significance. Known as Kura Tawhiti in the Māori tongue, which translates to 'treasure from afar,' Castle Hill is revered as a sacred site known as the 'birth-place of the Gods'. In the Polynesian tradition, the origin of humanity is deeply intertwined with the natural world. The primordial parents, Ranginui (the sky) and Papatūānuku (the earth), gave birth to Tāne, the forefather of humanity. Tāne created a woman named Hineahuone from mud, symbolizing the feminine essence arising from the soil. Hineahuone and Tāne had a daughter, Hinetītama. She served as the guardian of the boundary between darkness and light, dusk and dawn, revered both at sunrise and at sunset. Kura Tawhiti served as a kind of astronomical observatory for predicting seasons and weather patterns, with a considerable population from the coastal region migrating there during summer to tend the kumara crops and sweet potatoes. The limestone geology, believed to have been built up by ancient creatures since the dawn of time, was considered sacred and became a burial ground for prominent Māori leaders who first explored and inhabited the South Island. Its collection of gigantic stones, which seemed dropped from the sky by giants, inspired the once-visiting Dalai Lama to name it the 'spiritual center of the universe.' The creators of the 'dancing pictures' found inspiration in the magical world of C.S. Lewis and planted the Narnia realm here.

Around Castle Hill, the mountains are rocky and dry. The grass forms a deep, yellow cushion with barely any other vegetation, as if the wind dared any trace of a plant to stick its fragile stems out of the ground. But if you drive across the mountain pass, the orographic effect takes over, and the vegetation changes radically into a temperate rainforest. Through the windshield stretched the deep green of the enclosing forest, while the rear-view mirror reflected a stark world of yellow rock and dust. In front of you is Arthur's Pass, where the road crosses the mountains towards the verdant western coast. Nearby lies the spectacular Te Tautea o Hinekakai, the Devil's Punchbowl, a breathtaking cascade of weaving waters that seem to pour straight from the clouds, a divine fountain infusing the Māori spirit with life and vitality.

The road wound up and down through the verdant forest, untouched by civilization, with no sign of habitation for miles and miles. An almost ghostly farmhouse zipped by in our peripheral vision with a large Sméagol who sat on its roof. The new legends crept out of the forest, and a large Gandalf invited us inside for a dinner that we had already lost any hope of having in this desert of humanity, where even food seemed to be a legend.

The next morning on the western coast, we walked into a geological marvel of hundreds and hundreds of layers of deceased marine shells pushed by tectonic movements to the sea's surface. Punakaiki stands by the ocean, inviting the waves to crash underneath and to explode in spectacular blowholes. It resembles a layered cake of limestone, hinting at a stack of thin pancakes. Does its name come from its stackable appearance or from a Māori word meaning 'spring of food', a place of abundance known by the Māori travelers who paced the trails connecting the north part of the coast with Milford Sound? Their formation began roughly 30 million years ago, as lime-rich fragments of marine shells slowly accumulated on the ocean floor. Over eons, these remnants compressed and solidified, giving rise to the dramatic limestone towers and cliffs we see today, standing as silent witnesses to a bygone ocean world. They can still be seen taking shape at Punakaiki Beach, where shells and minuscule marine snails, layered like the intricate work of a meticulous artist, cover the rocks battered by the waves, laying the foundation of what would become, in millions of years, a new pancake rock. The atmospheric beach is where merging springs cascade as small waterfalls, tumbling from the rainforest into the Tasman Sea. These small brooks carve tiny caves, which collapse into gigantic and precarious grottos, shaped by the pounding of powerful waves.

PUNAKAIKI ROCKS, NEW ZEALAND

The spectacular rocks that stun travelers are only part of the massif formed around them. The surrounding cliffs steer your view towards a river valley, and you soon follow the Pororari River on its spectacular excursion through a canyon of layered rocks. The Punakaiki—Pororari River loop invites you to enter a mysterious rainforest. Its entrance is marked by three *waharoa* gateways carved by the Ngati Wawae clan as an entryway onto the track. The trail is ridden with gigantic ferns covering the path among contorted trees with moss hanging from their branches, little fantail birds zipping among branches, ear fungus mushrooms on the tree's bark looking as if the trees are listening to the sounds of the forest, whispering waterfalls and *kai-kai* or kidney ferns climbing toward the sky on the tree trunks whose peaks are lost in the dense canopy. We strayed a bit off the trail, only to have our shoes sink almost completely into a blanket of moss like a waving emerald sea.

"Where is this trail going? We had walked for an hour, and this place was sort of creepy. How long did you walk?" we were asked by several lost travelers coming our way on the trail. We wanted to say, "You are in the realm of Tāne, the revered Lord of the Forest," but we reverted to a mundane explanation pointing to the All-Trails map to keep them out of the mysterious legend.

As the eldest of six siblings, Tāne resented living in perpetual darkness, trapped between his celestial father, Ranginui, and his earthly mother, Papa-tū-ā-nuku. Yearning for light in his darkened world, he separated his parents, and in this monumental act, brought forth Te Ao Mārama—the world of light we inhabit today. But darkness is still the realm of many creatures. In hollow trees and rocks' hidden crags, tiny dots of light pierce the dark veil of the night. Silvery strings of fragile, rhomboidal, pearl-like worms hang in the humid climate, creating this spectacle. Their tiny glow lures their prey. Midges, mosquitoes, and moths get stuck on their sticky threads. The glowworm attracts the prey by generating through bioluminescence a dot of light on its tail, a glow that is a byproduct of its... excretion. But the spectacular speckles of light in the pitch dark of the forest cannot match the stunning view of the Milky Way in the southern sky when you watch it in the middle of nowhere. Or maybe we can think of that spectacle of myriad stars in the sky as a gigantic glowworm that created the world on which we humbly trample for a while.

CHAPTER 14

LOOKING FOR THE MISTY MOUNTAINS

TAI POUTINI NATIONAL PARK IS HOME TO NEW ZEALand's glaciers. Whatever you know about glaciers from other latitudes is turned upside down here, where temperate rainforest creeps towards the glacier's base, surrounding it in a verdant blanket. Franz Josef Glacier is known in the Māori tongue as Kā Roimata o Hine Hukatere. Legend has it that the name translates to 'the tears of Hine Hukatere' because, according to the oral tradition, Hine Hukatere's lover, Tuawe, perished in an avalanche while climbing the mountains with her. Overcome with grief, Hine Hukatere's tears cascaded down the mountainside. Seeing her anguish, the compassionate sky father Rangi froze her tears into a glacier and named it after her. Far better than the name of a distant European monarch.

Not far from it lies Fox Glacier—this time bearing the name of a New Zealand prime minister—but in Māori tradition, it is remembered with deeper resonance as the resting place of Tuawe. The pristine wilderness surrounding these glaciers shapes the allure of the place. We hiked through the rainforest, past old huts with relics of earlier explorations, beneath towering ferns and moss-draped trees, following a winding path that felt like a labyrinth built for giants, until we emerged at the glacier's moraine, revealed suddenly behind the sweep of a gigantic fern. High in the Southern Alps, known to the locals as Kā Tiritiri o te Moana, snow gathers in endless layers, compressing into ice that glides slowly yet relentlessly downhill. The glacier can advance or retreat as much as five meters in a single day, leaving behind the moraine on which we now stand.

Following New Zealand's west coast, south of the glaciers, Mount Aspiring is, according to the local legends, the resting place of Haast, a mythical bird with supernatural powers. It's a mountain of spiritual significance that links the earthly and spiritual realms, making the connection between Raki and Papa. Māori believe that Mount Aspiring is the younger brother of Aoraki (Mount Cook), the tallest mountain in New Zealand. It glitters brilliantly in the sun, living up to its Māori name, Tititea—'peak of glistening white'—a summit woven into the creation stories of the local *iwi*.

Driving through Mount Aspiring National Park along the Haast River is a journey through enchantment: snow-capped peaks rise like guardians, their presence felt from countless vantage points. Everywhere unfolds a procession of silvery cliffs, pristine rivers, plunging waterfalls, luminous blue pools, and serene lakes, all threaded together by trails that wind deep into the valleys, leading to remote huts scattered like quiet sentinels of the wilderness.

WANAKA TREE, NEW ZEALAND

After parting ways with the Haast River, the road clings to the shimmering contours of Lake Wānaka and Lake Hāwea, carrying us toward the dreamy little town of Wānaka, where the spell was broken by flocks of black crows that seemed to have claimed its alleys, beaches, and parks as their own. The place, covered in advertising for water activities and helicopter rides—they are everywhere in New Zealand -has a collection of restaurants, coffee shops, and ice cream parlors that all morphed the quietude of the glacier land and Mount Aspiring into a fleeting memory. But Wanaka looked charming with its beach full of people bathing in the warm waters of the lake. It was a place where, for sure, you felt like lingering and spending not a night but maybe a week, only to rest or find your way through the hiking trails that descend towards the lake. And as in many beautiful places I visited, that 'what if' hovered upon me. What if I just stay here for a while and not go back to the rat race of New York City? I walked by the lake on a trail that seemed to go on forever, lit by the scintillating reflections coming from the crystalline surface, and stopped for a moment to fill up my water bottle from a nearby fountain. In front of me was a guy whose long hair partially covered his tanned face. He was dressed in roughened jeans and an unkept T-shirt and was filling a larger-than-normal water jar.

"Wow, man, you must be quite thirsty..." I told him with a smile, trying to start a conversation.

"Yeah, I have to fill the water tank of that RV," he said, pointing to the nearby large camper parked on the street.

"Are you from here? Travel around?" I tried to place his accent, which didn't seem local.

"No, man," and lowering his face to see if the jar had filled up, "Not from here. I am from Montana."

"Oh! So you came on vacation and traveled in that RV? I saw so many RVs on the road. It seems that everybody has an RV here," I said.

"Actually, no," he said, taking the filled jar from the spout, "I stay here. I travel around and work here and there. Whenever I find some work... But you don't need a lot of money here. I came six months ago and plan to stay several more. Tomorrow we'll go to the fjords. Have you been there?"

"I love this... And the visa?" I said ignoring his question.

He turned to me, looking into my eyes for the first time. A smile on his face:

"Forget about that. I'll figure it out later. Just look around..." and raised his hand toward the lake and the surrounding mountain that seemed to pop out from another world. For God's sake, he was right! Why should you care about bureaucracy when there is so much beauty around?

Later in Queenstown, I got the same response, but this time from a local transplant. Two young guys, tanned and looking like college jocks, were barbequing some tomahawk steaks on a nearby terrace. We rented an apartment near them for several nights, enjoying the spellbinding views over Lake Wakatipu and the rocky peaks plunging into the lake. The guys were originally from Auckland and told us they rented the apartment and moved to Queenstown this summer. We talked about rents and apartment prices, though in reality, most units were taken by the constantly rotating carousel of Airbnb guests.

"So, why did you guys move here from Auckland? Was it anything with your job?" I asked. The guys smiled, the same smile as the guy from Montana.

"Why did we move here?" one said with a bemused look. "Why?!!" and he began laughing. "Just look behind!" he said, making a sign towards the lake and the peaks. "Where else can you find this?"

Light traffic makes driving in New Zealand a pleasure. The roads are in perfect shape due to a continuous repair effort, with one man or light controlling the traffic while others lay new pavement on parts of the road that would be considered very good in many other countries. Clusters of planted saplings cover entire hills or small patches of land, their fragile trunks protected by plastic cylinders that you can see from far away. They appear like traces of a misplaced human civilization in that primeval wilderness, yet serve a purpose in the struggle against deforestation. As the car sped along, we glimpsed farm after farm, each one dotted with sheep, pigs, cows, horses, deer, and even llamas.

You may encounter several conservation parks that save endangered species such as the Takahe bird, like the one we discovered in Te Anau. Not so endangered, unfortunately, were the annoying Namu sand flies. The small gnats will land on your body and pinch almost imperceptibly. You may not even notice them, but you will wake up in the middle of the night and scratch yourself to oblivion for weeks. But here we were in Fjordlands National Park on a glorious sunny day, so we forgot the damned flies having a feast on us.

From mind-boggling views of peaks among peaks seemingly clinging to the sky to magnificent waterfalls, to endless plains squeezed between mountains, to lakes perfectly mirroring the surrounding crests, to inviting tracks surrounding ridges and a mysterious tunnel guarded by flocks of kea on the road to Milford Sound, Fiordland is a collection of places so alluring that you keep stopping, feeling that you will never have time to reach its end. The drive through Fiordland to Milford Sound is considered the most scenic route in New Zealand.

In 1973, John Williams, then a geology student and now a professor at the University of Otago, inspired by Tolkien's *The Lord of the Rings*, proposed a fanciful list of new names for various places in Fiordland. Among the names were Mt Gondor, Rivendell Pass, Westernesse Pass, and Mordor Peak. He also renamed two other peaks, Sauron and Isengard Peak. The park's administration rejected the whimsical suggestions because they were not in tune with their nomenclature. Fast forward several decades, and Sir Peter Jackson arrived with his *Lord of the Rings* trilogy, dubbing the surrounding peaks 'the Misty Mountains' and the rest, as they say, is history. Nowadays, few visitors remember the English or the Māori names of the peaks, but all know how these places were named in the famous movie series.

MILFORD SOUND, NEW ZEALAND

In Milford Sound, we felt dwarfed by the surrounding peaks that seemed to crash over the boat we were in, not small at all if not by comparison. The sunny skies turned to clouds near the Tasman Sea, the most treacherous sea in the world, the curse of captains, many of whom left their bones on its bottom. On the shore, seals lay on rocks in the powerful wind that moves through the tree canopy hanging from the sheer cliffs, like a comb moving through hair. The forceful gale made the waterfalls flow upwards, defying gravity, as if they were climbing the mountain. Several times, the storms had destroyed the lighthouse at the end of the bay, forcing it to be rebuilt each time on higher ground, but to no avail. From here, several days to Tasmania, several weeks to Argentina. If you can make it...

According to the legend, Milford Sound was crafted by the divine hands of an *atua* (demi-god) named Tute Raki

Whanoa. With his *toki*, an ancient axe, and the power of *karakia* (prayer), he carved out the sharp valleys that define the scenery today and chiseled the rugged cliffs that surround it. The Māori named Milford Sound, Piopiotahi, which means 'only one *piopio*'. Another legend tells of the famous local hero, Maui, who, on a quest for mankind's immortality, met his demise at the hands of the goddess of death, Hine Nui TePo. Maui's partner, a *piopio*, a now-extinct small endemic bird, lamented his loss, singing a mournful melody in the Milford Sound, inspiring its Māori name. Captain James Cook sailed twice in 1773 near Milford Sound but failed to discover its entrance, never able to witness its grandeur.

We had a great sunny day in Milford Sound that enticed us to hike to Key Summit, part of the famous Routeburn Track, a 32 km track through an alpine landscape of remarkable beauty. Soon after we started the hike, clouds gathered, and an atmospheric fog enveloped the alpine shelf. Moss-covered trees, twisted as if by some unseen hand, morphed into ghostly shapes that seemed to close in on us from all sides.

CHAPTER 15

The Troll who Burned the Land

QUEENSTOWN STANDS ON THE SHORE OF LAKE Wakatipu, known in the Māori legends as the 'hollow of the sleeping giant.' It's a legend about the secret love between Matakauri, a young warrior, and Manata, the daughter of a Māori chief. One night, Matau, a giant taniwha, sort of a troll, kidnapped Manata and hid her in his mountain lair. This was the chance for Matakauri to prove his love. He went after Matau, killed him, and rescued and married the poor girl. The body of the dead Matau troll burned a hole in the ground, which soon filled with water, forming the large S-shaped Lake Wakatipu. Matau's body is stretched with his head towards Glenorchy and his feet at Kingston, while Queenstown sits on the giant's knee. According to legend, Matau's heart is the only part of the troll that remains alive, its rhythmic beating causing the lake's water level to rise and fall by 20 centimeters every 27 minutes. This phenomenon is called a seiche, and by a more mundane explanation, is caused by wind and atmospheric changes. Legend has it that the Hidden Island across the lake from Cecil Peak is actually the beating heart of the giant Matau.

Climbing the road up to the Remarkables ski resort, near Queenstown, rewards you with the most spectacular view of the lake. A short hike on its slopes and trails brought us to Lake Alta, an eye of emerald water surrounded by dry metamorphic rocks with intricate designs pushed up by the earth's pressure. While basking in the tranquility of the lake's serene environment, we were rattled by the sound of a helicopter. Despite the deafening noise, it was interesting to watch how the Kiwis were building a new ski lift, the entire work done by helicopters hauling materials. New Zealand is a sparsely populated country—just five million people over an area larger than the UK—yet its modern technology seems worlds apart from the legend of the giant said to have shaped Lake Wakatipu.

Driving towards the other end of Lake Wakatipu, we stopped at Puna Tapu (Sacred pool), an important place for Māori ceremonies. The Englishmen called it Bob's Cove, named after Bob Fortune, the commander of William Gilbert Rees' ship. Rees was an explorer, surveyor, and one of the first settlers in the Otago province of New Zealand. Considered the founder of Queenstown, Rees' statue adorns the pedestrian area of the town.

We kept driving towards the end of the lake and suddenly, on the side of the road, we saw the sign we were looking for. We read about Little Paradise Lodge in Atlas Obscura, but never saw it in another guidebook. Strolling through its gardens felt like stepping into a whimsical fantasyland, framed by the majestic Southern Alps. In its tiny parking lot, a VW Golf with sliced stones stuck over its entire surface welcomed us as a sign of what we might encounter later. Two circular gates made of driftwood—one adorned with a wire-meshed yellow butterfly, the other with a white peacock—stand like portals to another realm. Behind the gates were spiraled columns with signs made of flat pebbles pointing to various places on the globe, yoga poses statues shaped of dripped cement and covered in pebbles, and a giant, realistic spider web made from string, probably dipped in glue and covered in sand. A winding path guided us to a statue of a woman in a yellow dress, lifting a child by the arms and spinning him joyfully into the air. Nearby was a statue of a man battling a moa that was being attacked by an eagle. Among the statues were circles, arches, and spirals made of pancake rocks connected on their sides. Each patch of this fantasy land was adorned with scribbled quotes, making a connection to the world at large. On the side of a pond was a sign that could be read by viewing its reflection in the water. A spiral staircase ascended to the top of a tree, offering views of the Southern Alps, with branch-like banisters that avoided the straight lines of the modern world. *Whio*, the New Zealand endemic duck, as well as chickens and blue and white peacocks, roamed freely, and you were invited to feed them with food placed in containers by the side of the trail. It all ended in the guest bathroom, where fish swam in a tank above the toilet, surrounded by adobe walls and a sun-shaped mirror with driftwood rays. The sign by the sink read: 'Your hand washing water will be used in the toilet by the next guest'. Is this another realm that, by some accident, brushed against our world right here—precisely on the 45th parallel of the Southern Hemisphere?

WILD DREAM GARDEN, NEW ZEALAND

Thomas came to welcome us. Looking like a slightly tamer version of The Hobbit's Radagast with a beetle in his long hair and surrounded by bees, Thomas exuded a sense of freedom and *joie de vivre* that you'd hardly find even in New Zealand. He pointed to the stones around:

"People used to fight with stones. They threw some stones back and forth, and the fight was over. Now they push a button, and a city is gone. You feel embarrassed belonging to the human species. There are 8.7 million life forms on this planet. But we act as if this planet belongs to us. It does not. Nobody behaves the right way. We have to learn to share."

Thomas is an environmentalist. He had come from Switzerland many years ago, where he worked as a forest warden, and settled on the South Island. He told us how despondent he felt when he returned to Switzerland after many years and saw "what they did to their pristine environment." After some coffee and cookies, he invited us to the house whose front wall and columns were covered entirely in pine cones. The interior walls were covered in pebbles, creating convoluted designs or murals. The pebble design extended to the bathroom and its tub, where the modern faucets were barely visible, shyly sticking out of a design of dry roots covered in moss. The house's furniture was made of polished, recovered wood. Hangers were branches, tables were made of one wood, chairs out of tree trunks, and the entire floor was covered in planks of wood, polished and perfectly fitted. On one wall, a spectacular, large weaving, "the only one I ever made". Everything else, the house, its interior, and all the artifacts inside and in the garden, was made by Thomas with his own hands.

"We use more and more oil for a continuously increasing population that may not need it in the near future," he said, pointing to some charts etched in stone in his garden about yearly oil consumption around the world.

"And politicians and businesses want more and more. They probably pretend they are on opposite sides, forcing us to take sides. But maybe they just sit together and decide the life of the rest of us, who are just the idiots in this game. And now, as long as they have AI, they won't need so many people. We need to protect ourselves because at one point they may want to get rid of us," he said.

"We read articles about America's techno billionaires who buy New Zealand citizenship and build bunkers to shield themselves. It seems they are afraid of a major revolt because of this ridiculous income inequality. Do people here talk about this? Do you know where they built those bunkers?" I asked.

"I don't know. I wouldn't know," he said and stomped the ground laughing, "But doesn't it sound hollow?" and continued:

"I came here and left everything behind. It was great, of course. My youth and what this country had to offer. Its nature was unmatched, incredible. The grass just seems greener here, but it's not. Here, there are not enough people. The Department of Conservation sprays entire areas by helicopter to control the invading species. Instead of spraying each small patch of land separately, they destroy everything in the area."

On all the trails we tramped, we could see traps for rodents and weasels that weren't indigenous to New Zealand but imperiled the bird habitats by attacking nests and eating their eggs. The rangers closed the trails, and often you could hear the roar of the helicopters spraying a treatment against the rodents. Helicopters were everywhere, helping chop down dry trees, eyesores in manicured botanical gardens, landing tourists on glaciers for a quick photoshoot, or surveilling canyons and mountain peaks in short trips from most of the towns.

Thomas paused for a bit as if he had lost his train of thought:

"So, you like it here?" he asked, laughing, seeing how mesmerized we were by everything. "On holiday, it's always nice. I felt the same when I came here. I was young and restless and wanted to go far from civilization. And I came here and loved all of it. But never underestimate how comforting it is to have a shoulder to cry on. And now, when you grow old, you have almost nobody around."

We said goodbye to Thomas and his spectacular Wild Dream Garden and, continuing our drive, we finally made it to Isengard, where the Númenóreans in exile built the fortress meant to protect Gondor's northwest border in *The Lord of the Rings* trilogy. Actually, Glenorchy/Isengard is a charming place where the Dart River flows into Lake Wakatipu. The river serves as a conduit to Te Koroka, a mountain in Mount Aspiring National Park, rich in *pounamu,* the jade-like greenstone highly prized by the Māori. It is abundant in this part of Aotearoa, as the Māori call the land we know as New Zealand.

CHAPTER 16

MĀORI

WHILE TRAVELING IN THE SOUTH ISLAND, YOU GO round and round Aoraki/Mount Cook. It's always there but somehow unreachable. To come close to it, you have to go around the whole western mountain chain and drive the last leg from Queenstown, skirting the celestial blue surface of Lake Pukaki. And if the weather cooperates, Aoraki will shed its mysterious veil and you will be able to see it from afar in its full splendor. You can almost reach its base following Hooker Valley, a trail that crosses the Hooker River three times on suspended bridges that sway precariously in the gusty winds. The peak's base lagoon was filled with ice floats that broke loose from the glacier. We wanted to explore further, but the howling wind whispered that we should give up, so we sat at the base of the mountain, savoring its furtively offered splendid view—a gift soon to be veiled by the approaching storm. The mountain's southern face was the training ground for Sir Edmund Hillary's Everest ascent. The mountains' height is half that of Mount Everest, but it offers as many challenges.

MOUNT AORAKI, NEW ZEALAND

According to the ancestral legends of the Ngāi Tahu *iwi,* Aoraki and his three brothers trace their lineage to Rakinui, the Sky Father. The siblings descended from their celestial realm in a majestic canoe to visit Papatūānuku, the Earth Mother, and embark on an expedition across the vast expanse of land and sea. During their voyage, tragedy struck as their *waka* (canoe) foundered upon a treacherous reef, forcing the brothers to seek refuge atop the vessel's upturned hull. Their fishing proved fruitless, and hunger soon gnawed at their spirits, compelling them to contemplate a return to the heavens, to the sanctuary of their father. Aoraki had to initiate the sacred incantation to launch their colossal *waka* back towards the cosmic expanse, but hesitated to utter the final words that would liberate them from the earthly realm. Exposed to the merciless chill of the southern winds, Aoraki and his two other siblings turned into three majestic towering mountains, and the canoe metamorphosed into the South Island.

According to another Māori legend, Maui, armed with an ancestral jawbone hook, hauled a colossal fish from the depths of the sea. Together with his brothers, they hoisted the catch to the surface, which turned out to be a piece of land that formed the North Island, Te Ika a Māui. The South Island, named Te Waka a Māui, symbolizes Maui's *waka* anchored by Rakiura (Stewart Island), whose name translates as 'Māui's Anchor Stone.'

Between these islands, the strait named in modern times in Captain Cook's honor peeks out from a collection of fjords, from where sailboats and tugboats came out in the caressing sunset. We made the crossing, once done by Māori in *waka*, and boarded a large ferry where shiny cars glittered in the orange sunset. In three hours, we arrived at Wellington harbor on the North Island in closer proximity to the Māori *iwi* that until now we had encountered only through legends.

In Tolkien's famous trilogy, the Ring was forged within Sammath Naur, the Chamber of Fire, deep within Mount Doom, the volcanic stronghold of Sauron, who projected into its essence his formidable might. Mount Doom, the heart of Mordor, is in real life Tongariro National Park's Mount Ngauruhoe, a lava-covered volcanic cone considered sacred by the Māori. According to local tradition, Ngātoroirangi, a revered high priest, ascended Mount Tongariro with the intention of claiming all lands he could see from its summit. However, when he reached the peak, he was engulfed by a brutal, icy blizzard. Desperate and near death, he cried out to his ancestral spirits and his sisters in Hawaiki, pleading for fire to save him. To strengthen his spiritual call, Ngātoroirangi sacrificed his slave, Uruhoe, casting him into the crater. In response, fire surged across the land from Hawaiki, finally reaching the freezing priest on Tongariro's slopes. The mystical fire burned inside the crater, consuming Uruhoe's body in its flames. That crater came to be known as Ngauruhoe, meaning also 'throwing hot stones', a fiery tribute to the slave whose sacrifice secured the fire that saved Ngātoroirangi.

Jumping out of the legends, both Mount Ngauruhoe and Mount Ruapehu can be admired from the famous Alpine Crossing, considered the best day hike in New Zealand, passing through a valley covered by huge lava boulders rolled there by the last eruption of Mount Doom/Ngauruhoe. No, not the one from the movie though…

We began our hike on this desolate landscape inhabited by spirits and surrounded by mysterious mountains veiled in clouds that seemed to be pulled out of Tolkien's story. Hiking in New Zealand fills you with a deep admiration for the beauty nature can offer. Pure splendor, wonder, and reverence. You also develop a profound appreciation and respect for the remarkable stewardship and care the Kiwis have for their country and its spectacular landscapes.

When hiking on the numerous national park tracks, a flash of artificial color left on the ground strikes your attention, making you stop. It's just a tiny bit of blue plastic or maybe a piece of a bag taken by the wind that baffles you because this is such a rare occurrence, and for a moment, you feel that you have uncovered a new world, a world that we call civilization, which unravels in front of you by accident. But you may hike for days and not see any trace of human civilization despite the hordes of tourists that tramp New Zealand's national parks. In a recent story published by an

American newspaper, a reporter recounted how a catamaran captain dove into the water to retrieve a beer can he spotted floating fifty feet from shore—another example of New Zealanders' deep respect for nature and commitment to protecting the environment. Most of the trails that traverse the alpine terrain are built on boardwalks covered with wire mesh, guiding hikers across wet sections while safeguarding the fragile ecosystem. Numerous huts pepper the mountains, simple cabins with spotless bunk beds that must be booked in advance, manned by a ranger looking like he just popped out of *The Lord of the Rings*.

Unfortunately for us, the hikers descending from the top of the Alpine Crossing arrived completely drenched, straight out of the cloud that veiled them in a blanket of drops, and they advised us to turn around. So, we settled only for a partial discovery of the land of Mordor, waiting for sunnier days.

WAIMANGU VOLCANIC VALLEY, NEW ZEALAND

If we missed the fires of Mordor, we found others ablaze in the Waimangu Volcanic Valley, a place that bears witness to the power of boiling magma. The crater lake boils, raising vapors that float like a veil of clouds on its surface, offering a hellish image from above.

At the end of the valley, across a vast lake, rises Mount Tarawera, well known in New Zealand for its catastrophic 1886 eruption, which sent a towering ash column soaring some 10 kilometers into the sky. Earthquakes and thunderous explosions reverberated throughout the region. A rift, stretching 17 kilometers in length, tore through the mountain and surrounding terrain, burning villages and changing the landscape. The pink and white terraces, once the crowning jewels of New Zealand, were swallowed by the earth and by Lake Rotomahana that expanded in the aftermath of the eruption.

The Māori's life around this area has always taken place on boiling magma. In Whakarewarewa village of Rotorua, descendants of the chieftains who once led the *iwi* and governed the region, conduct tours, sharing in detail the rich traditions and history of their people. Their village lies on boiling ground with transparent blue pools that spit steam and scalding water. For generations, they had called this dangerous land home and had mastered the use of its vast subterranean energy for warmth and cooking.

The heart of the village is the *marae*, or the Māori meeting ground, and in its middle is the *wharenui*—a large house—an elaborately carved structure serving as a communal gathering place that plays a central role as a meeting place and ceremonial site. Known as *whare whakairo*, or 'carved house,' this style of construction appeared in the early to mid-1800s. *Wharenui* have elaborate carvings, both inside and out, featuring stylized depictions of the *iwi*'s ancestors whose styles and motifs vary from tribe to tribe. During formal Māori gatherings, they receive visitors with a ceremonial *hongi,* where noses are pressed together in greeting. Recitations in the Māori language, traditional songs, and a haka—the original war dance, now often performed to welcome visitors—are common, as are meals cooked on preheated stones in earth ovens called hāngī, adding cultural significance to the food.

WHAKAREWAREWA VILLAGE'S CEMETERY, ROTORUA, NEW ZEALAND

Māori society was formed by clans or *iwi* and is divided into three main social classes, or grades, that determine rank and status. Rangatira is formed by the chiefs and ruling families, Tūtūa were the commoners, and Taurekareka were the slaves. A Taurekareka can marry a Tūtūa and upgrade his status, but it is hard to reach further up. Even today, most, if not all, the Māori politicians are part of the Rangatira class.

Traditional Māori beliefs are deeply rooted in Polynesian culture, encompassing concepts like *tapu* (sacred) and its opposite, *noa*. Certain objects, entire areas, or buildings are considered *tapu* and require a special ceremony to convert them to *noa*. For example, a purification ceremony performed during fishing ensures the catch will not have *tapu* and can be killed and eaten. *Mana* is a central concept in Māori society, representing spiritual power, authority, and prestige, often inherited or earned through deeds, leadership, and ancestral lineage. Māori also have the concept of *wairua*, which is the spirit that connects people and shapes their ceremonies, daily practices, and rituals, emphasizing that life has more than a physical dimension. However, nowadays most of the Māori adhere to a form of Christianity.

The newly discovered business sense of the Māori was shaped with an emphasis on preserving the tribal tradition and cultural heritage, halting the unchecked development that had happened in many other parts of the world. Their careful stewardship likely tempered the *Pākehā*'s relentless drive for development, but together they forged a national consciousness that helped preserve the treasure they all inherited in this magnificent land. That awareness extended to the Kiwi way of life—calm, relaxed, and always ready for a chat wherever you meet them. And for a chat, a good cup of coffee is available everywhere. All supermarkets and all gas stations have baristas who make you the best possible cappuccino you've ever had with the tastiest beans that you'd ever find anywhere else. So, just relax and enjoy the coffee in Aotearoa's clean air.

CHAPTER 17

LANDING IN PARADISE

"YOU LOOKED COOKED!" JANE SAID WHEN I ENTERED the residential gate in the afternoon after an all-day hike on the island. I probably looked completely clueless about my appearance, as she continued: "Go and look in the mirror!"

I did, and, yes, I could see my face and head, a cherry red that would have raised the envy of a lobster. She went into the garden, plucked an aloe vera leaf, and started to help me heal my face. Jane was from Colorado. I met her in the residence the previous evening when I arrived, hanging out with a bunch of travelers in the yard. We all chatted in the morning like we'd known each other for ages at the lavish common breakfast laid out on a table in a garden that looked like the one from Eden. The large courtyard was full of tropical plants competing for space and sun, spearing their delightful flowers towards the light of a torrid sun. I invited Jane to hike around the island with me, but she had other plans, so I set off alone to explore.

I had landed on Easter Island the previous night on a flight that came from Santiago only three times a week. I had already traveled around South America for a month spending a lot of time in Patagonia, Chile and Argentina, a land that in my childhood, if it existed, a thing I was not sure of, I always associated with the most remote place in the world; a place I heard mentioned when somebody, pestered by constant questions of "Where are you going?" would finally say, "I am going to Patagonia!" So, in my mind, Patagonia, if it existed, was probably so far away that nobody wanted to live there. But when I arrived in this no-man's-land, I found just the opposite, with hiking trails that looked like city boulevards and sold-out glacier cruises with crowds of tourists disgorged by huge buses and vans. So, was there any place in this world that remained untouched?

While traveling through South America, hopping between Chile and Argentina on LAN and Aerolíneas flights, I found myself recalling the stories of Easter Island that had captivated me as a child. If I were here, so close to this enigmatic island, how about I go and see if there are any of those mysterious statues left standing, and maybe they can whisper in my ear some of their stories?

I landed at Mataveri Airport after a five-hour flight over the blue Pacific, wondering how, without GPS, you could find that 63-square-mile triangular spit of land in the immensity of the ocean. The airport consisted of only one runway, a pretty long one extended by the Americans to be used as a secondary runway for the space shuttle. We took our luggage and passed by a sign pointing to 'Easter Island' as if there were many other possible destinations in this splash of paradise. We walked on the tarmac to a modest building whose open windows were covered by reed screens to keep the rain away during storms. The airport 'terminal' was one large room with numerous tables where local women placed beautiful pictures of their rooms for rent. I randomly chose one and accompanied a lady to her van, then drove to a Garden of Eden brimming with flowers and tropical plants. Beneath a leafy canopy stood a table, used daily to serve house guests a copious breakfast of tropical fruits, fresh juices, and coffee. My new neighbors, mostly European and American travelers, shared stories of their daily hikes, sipping beers while briefly chatting about the trips around the island. I realized that, with stamina, I could walk everywhere by myself. However, it was not the effort but the relentless sun that cooked me during my exploration in a place where sunscreen was not a concept.

Somehow, I grew up with the legends of Easter Island, a place so remote and intangible, but always close to my curiosity. My curiosity was fed by the curiosity of others who reached this forsaken land and tried to untie its mystery. It all began in my childhood while watching a delightful Sunday morning TV series about a crew on a sailboat navigating the Pacific who discovered a mysterious tablet inscribed with an undeciphered script, coveted by a villain. Later, Thor Heyerdahl, the renowned Norwegian explorer, determined to validate his theory of migration patterns, wrote several books about his fascinating journeys. As a teenager, I would have loved to be part of his explorations. On top of all this, countless articles speculated that extraterrestrials had built the island's extraordinary statues, monuments unmatched anywhere else in the world. I had the feeling that way more was written about this island than about all the other Pacific territories combined, nudging me to believe that there is something special in this tiny piece of land in the most remote corner of the Pacific. Perhaps it was the last fragment of Lemuria, or the legendary continent of Mu, guarding the lost knowledge of the ancients. The most enthralling feature of this place may be its mythical dimension, with land, locals, and language all bearing the name Rapa Nui. The moment you step onto the island, legends pour in a deluge with contradictory facts, all passed down in the oral tradition of storytelling but retold with conviction based on documented facts etched in the volcanic tuff of the island.

Jorge was a Chilean from Santiago. Tall, with a long, suntanned face resembling the old Spanish conquistadors, he left his cosmopolitan life, settling on the island by marrying a local, Maria, the only way he could get his residency.

"Everything started with Hotu Matua. Did you hear about him?" he said while driving his battered van on the winding roads of the island.

I met him when he arrived in the morning to have coffee with our host in the garden, and I started asking him about the statues. I begged him to tell me the story and joined him on his errands that took us to several parts of the island.

"Hotu Matua was the king of Hiva, an island in the Marquesas. It's not exactly known which island, but this is what the legends say." And he continued

"Everything started from a dream where they saw some islands, actually a group of three tiny islands, and they left in canoes on an exploration to find them. And after they stumbled upon those islands, the king brought his people here, to Rapa Nui".

CHAPTER 18

THE *MOAI* THAT WALKED BY THEMSELVES

IT WAS NOT THE KING'S DREAM BUT THAT OF THE HIGH priest of Hiva, Hau Maka, whose spirit traveled across seas and meridians and could see from above the three small islands and 'a big hole' that was a volcanic crater. The traveling spirit continued his surveillance of the island's shore, naming twenty-eight places and marking several beaches surrounded by treacherous gulfs as good for landing. The spirit also marked this island as the eighth, and final island, in the twilight of the rising sun, naming it Te Pito O Te Henua, 'the navel of the world'.

The spirit in the dream told Hotu Matua to send two of his sons, together with Hau Maka's brother and five of his sons, on an expedition to find this place. They loaded their large canoe with yams, sweet potatoes, and bananas, and after five weeks at sea, they finally sighted the three small islands—Motu Nui, Motu Iti, and Motu Kao-kao—as well as the large crater of Rano Kao volcano. They landed on one of the island's beaches following the precise instructions given in the dream by the spirit. If you can employ such a spirit, forget about GPS navigation!

The hagiography of these first explorers was preserved in meticulous legends that recorded the names of the places they discovered, the exact days of their voyages, the actions of each member during the expedition, and even the precise methods they used to plant the vegetables they had brought—all in exacting detail. Hotu Matua arrived here later in a double-hulled canoe with his family and found a rocky island with few places ready for planting crops.

"But how come all this is known? Was this written in documents? Because, as far as I know, nobody could read those tablets' scripts!" I asked.

"This is how the legends were passed on through generations. Orally. Probably it is written, but, yes, you are right that we could not decipher the tablets. When all this happened, it's not exactly known," Jorge said, "The archeologists have several theories shifting the years of arrival from 300 AD to 1200 AD. The last period was somehow in tune with the Polynesian migration that populated the other islands of the Pacific."

And there is also the story of the Long Ears and the Short Ears," Jorge continued. From here on, the entire story becomes increasingly murky with competing theories contradicting each other. According to one of these theories, the island's colonizers, a semi-legendary elite, were called Hanau 'Epe. Stout and bulky, these fellows had elongated earlobes, almost to their shoulders, probably from wearing heavy earrings. Like Buddha, but less Zen. Later on, another wave of migrants arrived, a group of people of a slightly different race called Hanau Momoko, tall and slender fellows taking their name from *moko moko*, the Rapa Nui word for lizard. The two groups were known as the Long Ears and the Short Ears.

When you walk the island's trails, you end up in places where a large accumulation of rocks hints at an old *ahu,* a ceremonial place with statues spread around it. I came here to find these statues and see with my own eyes the mysteries that captured my childhood's imagination. They are named *moai,* which in the local language means *to exist,* and they were placed on top of an *ahu.* Some *ahu* were built on top of tombs that still contain bones. Others were built on a platform made out of perfectly cut stones that reminded me of Peru's Inca walls. This inspired Thor Heyerdahl to search for a connection between the island's early settlers and the civilizations of South America. Further away from the *ahu* is a terrace made out of small, round boulders gathered from the ocean.

"This place is called Ahu Akivi. It has seven *moai,* and they all look towards the sea. They were restored recently. They are unusual because, as you will notice when you explore the island, all the other statues look towards the interior, not towards the ocean." Jorge said.

Each *moai* represented a leader, an *ariki,* who ruled that section of the island for a generation. The statues, carved from gray tuff, sometimes wear a red hat called a *pukao,* made from a different type of volcanic lava. The headgear is not a hat but signifies the topknot, the traditional way the Polynesians gathered their hair. This part of the statue was quite important because, according to the locals' belief, the *ariki's mana* was stored in his hair. The tradition claimed that the community's survival was dependent on the leader's *mana,* his spiritual power. Even after the chieftain's death, his *mana* survived in the *moai* and was projected to the land for the benefit of the people who inhabited it. Archaeologists suggest this may explain why most *moai* face the interior of the island rather than the ocean.

"There's another legend, a newer one spread after they restored the statues in 1960, that says that Ahu Akivi's reversed orientation is because the *moai* look towards the Marquesa Islands from where Hotu Matua brought his people to Rapa Nui. I don't know where this came from, but it's another theory," Jorge continued.

There are many other *ahu* currently in disrepair, with one or more large *moai* toppled near them, some looking imploringly toward the sky with their *pukao* scattered around the sites. In Akahanga, there are the ruins of an ancient village. The remains consist of elliptical stone houses resembling canoes, where the floors and front porches are covered in the same round boulders used to cover the terraces in front of the temples. Near the boathouse are the remains of an old stone oven, and not far away is the cave used by the locals as a refuge during storms.

Ahu Akahanga is a large platform on which thirteen *moai,* averaging between five and seven meters tall, lie flat on the ground, both face-up and face-down. The once proud statues look despondent, ineffective in projecting their spiritual power as they lie flat in the volcanic debris. One of them is a small two-meter *moai* that may have been one of the first to be installed on this *ahu*.

"Ahakanga is very important in local tradition because, according to the legends, here is the burial place of Hotu Matua," Jorge said. "At his death, his sons took his body from his house on Rano Kau volcano and buried it here. And to make sure that the *mana* was preserved, they cut his head and buried it separately. The legend says that the head was stolen by a chieftain of the competing Ahu Te Peu clan to benefit from the *mana* imbued in the skull, just to be recovered later by the king's descendants." However, in a surprising move that the legends do not explain, Ahu Te Peu was the burial ground for Hotu Matua's sister.

"It seems that Ahakanga and Ahu Te Peu are lined up somehow astronomically".

Recent astronomical research has found that the two sites lie at the ends of an axis aligned with the sunrise and sunset of the summer and winter solstices—a connection that may have been known to the Rapa Nui of that era.

"But whether they knew or not, for sure it makes for a great story," as Jorge ended his own story.

Walking past platforms and toppled *moai* and listening to Jorge's stories, we finally arrived at Rano Raraku, an extinct volcano that served as the quarry for these impressive Rapa Nui *moai.* Rano Raraku exudes the feeling that this was the heart of the ancient Rapa Nui civilization. The place evokes an almost surreal sense of mystery, stronger than any other place on Easter Island. On the volcano's slope are scattered tens of abandoned statues, their heads sticking out of the ground. The collection of heads is spread in all directions, looking as if they are ready to walk down the mountain. This is exactly what the local tradition says: after they were carved, the statues got up and walked by themselves to their place on the *ahu,* the temple platform dedicated to a specific family that ruled over that part of the island.

Rano Raraku is a volcano, and its main stone is tuff, made from volcanic ash. A soft material, tuff, was preferred by the ancient Rapa Nui, who had no metal tools and used rocks to shape the monolith taken from the mountain. The tuff slabs were cut on the rocky side of the volcano at different levels, one over the other, like in a multiple-floor layered factory. From these slabs, the carvers shaped the statue *in situ*. Some of the statues have beards. Others have holes on their side as a sign of a tattoo. There are smaller *moai* representing females wearing earrings. There is one kneeling *moai* resembling the ones on Marquesa Island. Other *moai* have a boat graffiti etched on their chest, hinting at Heyerdahl, a connection with the Tiwanaku statues. But because of the softness of the tuff, all statues wore over time. In the quarry lie roughly 400 statues, some unfinished, some abandoned mid-creation, yet all among the most exquisitely crafted on the entire island. The carvers named *hotu* ran this place as a business, selling these statues. People came from all over the island to buy the *moai* from the sculptors, offering in exchange, food and other goods.

The first explorers who arrived on the island wrote in their journals about what were later known as the gigantic Easter Island heads. Later, it was discovered that most of the statues at Rano Raraku were buried between a third and a half into the ground, leaving only their oversized heads. Measuring inside the ground, the tallest statue in Rano Raraku has a complete height of 72 feet. I walked up to one of them, raised my arms, and asked Jorge to take a picture of me. In the picture, my hands barely reached the statue's chest. The bottom part of the body, buried underground, was actually used for managing their large weight. The workers detached the large body of the statue from the volcano quarry and, taking advantage of the inclination, pushed it down the volcano's slope, bottom first. On the way, they made a hole in the ground and pushed the bottom of the statue towards it. Gravity caused the statue to tilt forward, eventually settling upright in the pit, its base buried in the earth. *Hotu* carved statues like this for 400 years, first of small dimensions, but later larger, up to huge megaliths. Once the statue was purchased, the helpers dug the ground in front of the statue, and through techniques that are more guessed than known today, the statue was moved to the *ahu* where it would stand in the future. And if the statues were moved standing—hard to imagine how, but who knows—that method may have inspired the legend that the *moai* walked on their own, powered by their *mana*.

"The legends say the *moai* walked down the hill to their *ahu* on the island. Isn't it cool?" asked Jorge excitedly.

Some of these *moai* did not have to walk far because on the ocean's shore, right off the quarry, is Ahu Tongariki, the largest *ahu* on the island, with its fifteen generations of standing statues facing the interior of the island towards the rising sun. The 1960 powerful tsunami moved these *moai* one hundred meters inland from where decades later they were recovered with great effort by a Japanese crew and reassembled on their *ahu*. The 9.5-magnitude earthquake that devastated the village of Hangaroa also triggered a ten-meter tsunami, which surged up to 500 meters inland. The wave traveled 4600 miles through the Pacific, reaching Hawai'i and destroying the town of Hilo.

We left behind Rano Raraku, with its legends of the walking *moai*, just to be surrounded by horses running on the side of the road. You could see them trotting and gathering in groups around the island, maybe a symbol of the free spirit of the place.

"What's up with these horses? Who are their owners?" I asked Jorge.

"They are wild. Or better said, they became wild after their owners bought cars and decided they did not need them anymore. Everybody was on horseback on the island for generations, but now we all have pickup trucks. The horses were abandoned and left to themselves. It's nice to see them running like this. They seem so free and happy," said Jorge.

The cars were brought on a cargo ship that happened to arrive in the harbor just as we were speaking. The boat came every eight weeks, more often than a previous twice-a-year supply to the island. The loose horses roamed unhindered, their freedom echoing the islanders' unhurried way of life, a quiet communion with nature seldom found elsewhere.

On the northern side of the island, not far from Ovahe Beach with its pleasant sands, Te Pito Kura is a ceremonial complex of great archeological importance. Near the location of its *ahu* stands, toppled to the ground, the largest *moai* ever cut in Rano Raraku and mounted on a platform. The *moai* named Paro reaches 10 meters, weighing 80 tons, and its two-meter *pukao*, rolled despondently in front, weighs ten tons. Probably because of his large weight, this *moai* was one of the last to be toppled shortly after 1838, following the legendary wars between the clans.

"Look how big it is! Gigantic. Imagine how it looked standing tall here. But this is a special place. Unique! Go and put this on that rock," said Jorge, giving me a small compass and pointing to a rock nearby.

The ovoidal stone located a few meters away had impressive magnetic properties. According to the legend, the polished stone known as Te Pito Kura, or 'the navel of light,' was carried by Hotu Matua for its extraordinary *mana* when he navigated from Hiva to Rapa Nui. In the heat of the day, the compass became confused and kept spinning once I placed it on top of the iron-rich rock.

Passing by Ahu Heiki'i, the largest *ahu* on the island, with its three large *pukao* spread with impressive petroglyphs, we finally reached Anakena Beach, where Hotu Matua is said to have landed, founding the first settlement that would give rise to Rapa Nui culture.

"I have to go do some more errands. I leave you here. It's a nice place, so enjoy!" Jorge said.

"But how will I get home?" I asked him, a bit concerned.

"Don't worry about it. Just ask somebody and they will bring you to town," he said and waved goodbye.

Anakena is a stunning beach, evoking images of remote, dreamy Polynesian islands with palm trees whose fronds sway gently in the breeze. To add a unique exoticism to the place, by the beach is a line of seven recently restored *moai* standing on a platform shaped like a boat and named Ahu Nau Nau. Most probably, Hotu Matua loved this beach where he first landed because he chose it as the burial ground for his wife.

AHU NAU NAU, EASTER ISLAND

Ahu Nau Nau is the best-preserved site on the island, with almost intact statues extracted from the sand that conserved them. I started to walk around the statues and found the first four of them in perfect condition, crowned with a *pukao*, carved from the red volcanic rock of the Puna Pau quarry. The statues' surfaces, quite stylized and polished, had refined facial features, the first wearing an unusual conical *pukao*. On the buttocks of one *moai* was a sort of belt carved with geometrical figures and spirals that may have represented a tattoo.

In more recent excavations, pieces of white coral were discovered here that, put together, formed a white eye that fit perfectly into the *moai*'s socket, which, until then, was thought to have always been empty. According to the legend, these eyes were the projector of the *mana* stored in the *pukao*. There are lots of broken statue pieces around the ahu, hinting that there may have been eight or even more *moai* on the platform. The platform was carefully carved and had in it a *moai* head, laid horizontally, probably brought from another site on the island to add its spiritual *mana* to the ahu. On the back side of the platform, there is a series of interestingly carved petroglyphs of birds in flight, large-eared humanoid figures, and the mythological figure of *tangata moko* or lizard-man. Or maybe it represents a monkey symbolizing Tane, the god of the forest and birds, credited with shaping the first man, whose cult was widespread among the Māori of New Zealand. Archaeologists believe this *ahu* was constructed in three stages between 1100 and 1400 AD, though evidence suggests an earlier settlement on the beach dating back to 900 AD. Nearby on a large platform overlooking the sea stands a lonely *moai*, the first one re-erected on the island in modern times at the suggestion of Thor Heyerdahl, who, in his book *Aku*

Aku, describing his life on the island, encouraged the locals to re-erect the statues.

So, what happened to all these *moai*? Why were they toppled? Who were the ones behind the destruction, and what turmoil drove this upheaval? There were centuries of *moai* building, and out of the blue came this revolution that destroyed an entire culture.

I was lying down on Anakena Beach, enjoying the breeze and thinking about this unraveling past, most probably bloody. Locals were basking in the sun, while kids were playing ball on the beach or bathing in the ocean. It was an image of a paradise in a corner of the world seemingly forgotten by civilization. The surrounding carefree attitude was epitomized by a horse who drifted obliviously in his reverie and peacefully grazed in front of the seven *moai* while some of his equine buddies roamed among the palm trees. Suddenly, a local guy jumped on one of them and rode away. I took my backpack and started to walk along the road when a pickup stopped nearby.

"*A donde vas?* (Where are you going?)" The driver asked, making a sign for me to jump on and ride with them to the village. "Better stand up, but hold on tight to that bar because we drive fast," he said as he charged down the empty road towards Hangaroa.

In the evening, I asked my host where Jorge's house was, and I went to look for him. He was not back from his errands as I was told by a guy sitting on the porch.

"But what do you want with Jorge?" the man asked. I told him about the tour we had in the morning while he ran his errands, and the stories he told me, and I wanted to find out more.

"He told me everything about the *moai*, but I wanted to find out how and why the *moai* were toppled," I said

"Oh, I see. Stories from the past...What's your name? Where are you from?" he asked. I told him.

"I am Horatio, Jorge's cousin. I can tell you about that. Weird stuff though."

"But do you have time to chat? I just showed up like this...I really don't want to bother ..."

"No worries about time. We have time here." Horatio said, taking a sip from a beer that was on a table in front. "*Muchas historias, pero nadie lo sabe con certeza.* (many stories, but nobody knows for sure), and continued:

"There were two groups of people who lived in opposite parts of the islands. Either they came at the same time as Hotu Matua, or they came one after another from different places. Nobody knows for sure, but people talk like they know everything about it." Horatio stopped for a moment and took another sip from his beer.

"Some say that the *moai* were built by the Long Ears, but others say that both groups built them".

As the first inhabitants of the island, the Long Ears probably developed a pretense of godly origin. From it stemmed an aristocratic behavior and an arrogant right to rule over the island, designating all others as slaves. The Short Ears' revolt had been simmering for a while till a conflict peaked, and the Short Ears pushed the Long Ears towards the Poike volcano peninsula. Terrified by an imminent attack, the Long Ears dug a large ditch to protect themselves from the invaders. They filled the ditch with wood that they ignited, hoping to block the attack. But there was a traitor among them who showed the Short Ears another way down the coast, up from a cave on the shore, from where they could climb into the stronghold.

The attack of the Short Ears was merciless, pushing the Long Ears into their burning ditch where all of them perished. Tradition says that only one Long Ears survived the marasmus.

"But nowadays no Long Ears DNA can be found, so it's hard to say what is legend and what is not in this story," said Horatio.

Later on, Thor Heyerdahl developed the theory that the Long Ears migrated first from South America, and the Short Ears were brought as slaves in the 16th century.

"Who knows? The very timing of this possible war among the Ears is uncertain, historians placing it somewhere between 1500 and the late 17th century," said Horatio.

The story goes that the Short Ears took over and began their exclusive rule over the island. They started by destroying the elements of authority of the old way of living, the *moai*. Across the entire island, the *moai* were toppled in a revolutionary rage resembling similar dark moments of humanity far distanced from this forgotten corner of the globe, proving that people of all races and conditions share the same unpleasant behavior in comparable situations. In fact, this should actually make us more brotherly than we are...

The toppling of the *moai* is not retold in legends but was documented by European explorers, starting with Jacob Roggeveen, who arrived on Easter Sunday of 1722 and etched the new name of the island, Easter Island. Later, Captain Cook mentioned in his journal that during his 1774 voyage, most of the *ariki's* statues were standing. Fifty years later, other reports noted that only a few *moai* remained standing, to the point that the last standing statue was reported in 1831.

CHAPTER 19

Birdman is not just a Movie

ON THE OPPOSITE SIDE OF THE POIKE PENINSULA IS Rano Kao, another volcano of Rapa Nui, on whose rim Hotu Matua built his residence with spectacular views of the three tiny islands that came up in Hau Maka's dream. One day, I decided to walk over there and hike around the volcano's crater. The previous evening, I had gone to see Jorge and Horatio again, hoping to hear more stories from them. They were having a good time downing some beers and invited me to join them. However, they were less eager to chat about legends, immersed in a more mundane discussion about an issue with a pickup truck's transmission. They responded to a few of my questions without much enthusiasm, directed me to Orongo to find out about the birdman, and then soon returned to the topic of the gripped transmission. I thanked them for the beer and left for my residence.

Exactly as described in Hau Maka's dream, Rano Kao volcano was a big hole, surrounded by an almost uninterrupted rim, inviting exploration. The crater floor was covered in totora, resembling an abstract painting, with patches of green algae scattered across the still water. I hiked slowly around the crater, reaching its peak in the village of Orongo, from where I had a perfect panorama of the three tiny islands.

Here in Orongo began the second part of the Rapa Nui story. If it were a movie, this could be the sequel. The village was the residential place of the Rapa Nui royalty of this part of the island. It consisted of several windowless houses with large patios between them, once used for ceremonial dances and rituals. The houses had rounded stone walls with low doors and vaulted ceilings covered by flat grass roofs, recently renovated in what is now a national park. Nearby lay a rock quarry, the source of the stone used for the buildings. There were also red slabs with petroglyphs representing a man with a bird head and figures of *Make Make,* a single divinity added as the supreme god of the Rapa Nui's Tangata Manu sect that followed the *moai* cult period. *Make Make* was the creator and fertility god, depicted with a face featuring large eye sockets and a huge mouth that collected rainwater. He seemed to have replaced Tano, the god of fertility for the Māori of New Zealand.

After the battle that eliminated their opponents, the Short Ears had to establish a new order for ruling the island, so the local clans thought about a fairer way to designate a leader of this new society. They developed an annual competition called Tangata Manu, or the Birdman, in which the winner would be recognized as leader for the coming year. In this way, hereditary leadership gave way to a new form of governance, with power rotating among the clans. Most likely, the rise of this new cult triggered the destruction of the *moai,* which were seen as relics of the old order. Their *mana*, once central to the community, had to vanish to make space for the new faith to take root.

On an island with no large mammals or reptiles, birds were the only living creatures close to humans. The belief was that the birds had connections with the gods as long as they shared the sky with them. One of these migratory seabirds was manutara, a sooty tern, the bird that, in the locals' imagination, connected the earth, the sea, and the sky, coming to lay its eggs in the three small islets that appeared in Hau Maka's dream. This bird was known as orongo, or the 'messenger of peace' in the local language. The bird's arrival was also a celebration of fertility, honoring the god *Make-Make*, who was believed to have brought this bird from Hiva, the land where it nested each spring.

BIRDMAN PETROGLYPHS IN ORONGO VILLAGE AND THE THREE ISLANDS, EASTER ISLAND

During the festivities of choosing the new Tangata Manu leader, the chiefs of the most important clans gathered at the base of Rano Kau volcano. The event was marked by large feasts, traditional dances, and sacrificial rituals involving victims from rival clans, sometimes including acts of cannibalism. Meanwhile, the *ivi Atua* (priests) chose young servants, named *hopu manu,* to represent their clan in the competition. In July, all the *hopu manu* climbed the volcano's slopes and arrived in the village of Orongo, where they stayed in the 54 stone houses. The priests sang praises invoking *Make-Make,* their verses perhaps once etched onto the *rongorongo* tablets known as *kohau kiri taku ki te Atua* in a script that remains undeciphered to this day. The arrival of the supreme leader Ariki Henua signaled the start of the competition with all the *hopu manu* descending the almost 300-meter vertical cliff towards the shore. From there, using a reed float called *pora,* they began swimming towards Motu Nui, the largest of the three islets that appeared in Hau Maka's dream and which could be seen from the Orongo village. The ones who made it, evading the sharks and the treacherous surfs, had to find shelter in the caves of the Motu Nui shore, waiting days or even weeks for the manatura bird to show up and lay eggs. When at last the birds arrived and began laying eggs, the *hopu manu* who seized the first one sprinted to a sacred rock and shouted down toward a cave at the cliff's base. He would mention his leader's name and the expression *ka varu te puoko,* which means 'shave your head'. After that, the young servant tied the egg with a band on his forehead and began swimming frantically back to the shore, climbing back up the treacherous rocks to the Orongo village and offering the intact egg to the leader of his clan, who became the *tangata manu,* the birdman, for the next year. The competition's success was announced by lighting a fire on the rim of the volcano.

The new *tangata manu* was the receiver of the *mana* offered by *Make Make*. To be recognized, he had to shave his head, wear a wig, and be painted in the ritual colors of red and white, after which he could start his march across the island. In Orongo, petroglyphs representing the Birdman, with the body of a man and the head of a bird, might have been drawn as an offering to *Make Make*. This Orongo symbol can also be found on some of the remaining *moai*, with the Birdman engraved on their backs. Did these numerous petroglyphs represent the number of winners of the competition? We will never know exactly.

Tangata manu was considered *tapu* (sacred), and no one was allowed to approach him. To keep him out of sight, he stayed in a house built specifically for him in Anakena or Rano Raraku, spending his time with a priest who was there to serve all his needs. After one year, he was allowed to return to his clan, who venerated him because the sacrifice of his past year's boring life offered great benefits and privileges to the entire clan, mainly in the form of control of the island's food supply.

Of course, once a clan won these privileges, they had no intention of letting them slip away, and before long, the victors were plotting how to cling to power. They excluded rival clans from the competition, increased the number of birdmen chosen each year, provoking internecine conflicts tinged with cannibalism, and gradually stripped the ritual of its original significance. The coming of Catholic missionaries in 1867 brought the birdman competition to an end, with the last *tangata manu* chosen about a century after the tradition began.

But together with the missionaries who came to the island, the slave traders from Peru—themselves good Catholics but business is business even in the service of Jesus—started snatching locals and selling them as slaves to other places. The situation became so desperate that the missionaries petitioned the Chilean government for help, and the government sent its navy to the island, practically conquering it. Soon after, the Chilean government ordered the relocation of all locals in the village of Hangaroa and gave the island in concession to a Scottish sheep breeding company, which used the local people almost as slaves. The terrible situation lasted until the 1960s when the concession was voided, and the island was reopened, allowing the locals to return to their original settlements.

I was absorbed in this grim but strangely compelling history. The legends appeared to spring from a secret wisdom, worlds apart from the many European books about the island, each telling its own version of the story. In his delightful book *Aku-Aku,* Thor Heyerdahl recounted numerous stories about his life on the island, describing the toppled *moai,* the caves hiding skulls and bones, and even the Catholic Mass at Hangaroa church. During my solitary walks around the island, I was thrilled to discover the caves and see the skulls still intact, and to join the inspiring mass at the local church. The music was played on mandolin and guitars, and the churchgoers' choir sang in the Rapa Nui language. The entire community was there, old and young, all praying, all smiling, happy to be filmed, chatting among themselves while enjoying their paradisiacal life. Time usually changes things, but on this island, somehow, time stopped. I felt that I was part of a time before I was born, an impossible time in the world of planes and fast communication, where everything is known, creating a boring uniformity. When I visited Rapa Nui, the fast-paced world had not yet fully imposed its tendency to make every place look the same. There was no Internet on the island, an Internet that, at the time, was still spreading across the world via modems. All over the island, I met people who recounted bits and pieces of this story, between van rides, taxi trips, hitchhiking, or perched in the backs of pickup trucks. To see and hear it all, I walked for several days everywhere on the island from HangaRoa to Rano Raraku, to Anakena, and again back to Te Pau, to Rano Kau, and back to Poike in the sweltering heat of the day that burned my skin and made me look like a lobster.

Thus, I received this fascinating story, preserved here exactly as the locals have told it for centuries through traditional oral storytelling. They told me to pass it on to my children and to others interested in hearing it. The more I heard parts of the story, the more I realized that I would forget bits of this convoluted collection of legendary facts. Thus, on the day I ascended to Orongo village, I resolved to record myself on camera, recounting the story with every detail I could recall. I placed the camera on a tripod and told the story with the camera facing the three small islets of the *Tangata Manu* competition that appeared in a millennium-old dream.

CHAPTER 20

At the Jail on Easter Island

WHEN I DESCENDED FROM ORONGO, THE HEAT WAS overwhelming, and all I wanted was to sit under a palm tree by the beach and escape it for a while. I kept walking through the sweltering day until, at last, a restaurant terrace appeared nearby. I ordered a *cerveza fría* and let the gentle breeze, rustling the palm fronds, accompany it. Sipping the cold beer, it regretfully dawned upon me that the days in paradise are always numbered, and eventually the plane would carry me away to Santiago later today.

The down-to-earth feeling was forced upon me by a frantic morning call from Long Island: the driveway was covered by a thick layer of snow, and the car could not be pulled out to go to the supermarket. Snow? Supermarket? For a moment, I could not even understand what it was all about. Why was this an issue when you could just go and pluck a ripe fruit from the garden? This first-world problem was almost impossible to grasp here, striking me as something from another world. With great effort, like waking from a profound dream, I was able to make some suggestions on how to manage the snow situation.

On my last day in paradise, quenching my thirst with the cold *cerveza,* looking towards the blue of the ocean, there was a *moai* on one side of the terrace who was looking at me like he also wanted a cold beer. I sipped my beer quietly. The waitress came to ask if I wanted another or anything else.

"I am fine for the moment. *Gracias.... Pero....*" and a thought came to my mind.

"By any chance, do you know a place where I can buy some *artesania.* I went to the market and bought a piece, but I wanted to look somewhere else."

I wandered through the Mercado de Artesanías, a charming market teeming with artists and their statues, yet I couldn't help noticing how tightly managed everything seemed. The woodwork was great, but a few pieces were outstanding.

"*Si, no problema,*" says the waitress. "*Mi amor Pepe es un artesano,* and he makes lots of objects. And his pieces are less expensive than the *artesanos en el mercado.*"

"Oh, this is great. Can I go to see him?" I responded enthusiastically, ready to depart.

"*Siguro.* You have to go to the jail and tell him that his *novia* Cristina sent you there," she tells me in the most natural tone, like saying that Pepe just slept in a hammock on the back porch. I paused for a moment to make sure I understood correctly.

"*A la carcel?* (to the jail)" I asked

"*Si. No está lejos.* (it's not far)." She said if this was the main hurdle. "Just walk on the road and in 10 minutes you'll get there. You'll see a flag on a tall post." Cristina told me with a big smile.

My mind started to spin, juggling the impossibilities. Obviously, I could not go there! That's clear. How would I go to the jail and request to see an inmate? On Easter Island, of all places? How do you even make that request? Would we have to meet in one of those glass-separated rooms with phones, like I saw on *The Wire*? But how could he sell anything from the jail to an outsider? Or perhaps he's a guardian, moonlighting by selling pieces of *artesanía*? Should I ask her if he is an inmate or a guardian? Or should I ask her what he did to end up in jail in this paradisiacal place? It might not sound nice to her. But what difference does it make? I was imagining myself going to Rikers Island in New York and asking one of the officers dressed in a dark uniform adorned with guns, handcuffs, and pepper spray around his belt about an inmate who sells 'I love NY' T-shirts. What would the NY officer say? Would he give me a high-five or a fist bump? Most probably it would be a

Sir, we do not give any information about the inmates.

Yeah, but he is an artist and I want to meet him.

Would he say: *Why didn't you say so? Talented inmates always receive special treatment from us. Please come in.*

No way. He would kick me out in a rush, and the huge doors would bang behind me. However, the idea bugged me, and I thought, OK, I will only walk in that direction and see where the jail is. So, I paid for the beer and told Cristina I'd go to jail, though I knew there was no way I could actually meet her fiancé.

"Tell Pepe that I love him," she waved to me. Sure, Cristina, I will tell him, if I don't end up there myself after I try to meet him.

I had about two hours until I had to go to the residence to pick up my luggage and go to the airport on my last day in paradise. Why do I want to ruin everything by risking ending up in jail? The town's main road was flanked by houses with gardens, interspersed with empty lots. Wild horses were roaming while a few cars could be seen driving on the narrow road. I was again walking in the island's heat, surrounded by flowers and luxuriant vegetation. I kept walking for about 15 minutes when, on the left side, I saw the Chilean flag. Behind the flag post, there were some small mud barracks with tiny windows. Everything was spotless, with trees lime-painted up to the middle, reminiscent of a military garrison in Eastern Europe.

Ok, I am here. Now what? I walked sheepishly, pretending to be a tourist who lost his way and arrived at the gate. The padlock was open, but the heavy bolt was jammed in place. I decided to knock on the gate to see what could happen.

"*Are you sure you want to go there*?" my consciousness nudged me.

I knocked again. Still nothing. It was hot, and siesta time on the island, so most probably everybody was sleeping. I struggled to open the bolt, and when it finally gave way, the squeak of the hinges roused a guardian. He emerged from a side house, his short pants unzipped, carrying a belt in his hands. Now was the big moment. What should I say?

"*Hola. Es esta la cárcel?* (Is this the jail?)" I asked as if I were someone looking for the Statue of Liberty.

"*Si, señor,*" he told me, trying with no luck to insert the belt that would have stopped the gravitational tendency of his pants.

"*Oh, bien*...*Estoy buscando a Pepe* (I am looking for Pepe)," I said as naturally as possible—after all, who else could I look for?

"*Oh, Pepe. Siguro. Un momentito*......*Pepee!*" he screamed from the depths of his lungs, "*alguien te está buscando.*"

From the front barrack with tiny windows, a guy, awakened by the commotion, stumbled out. Immediately after him, another shirtless guy pulling up his short pants came out.

"*Yo soy Pepe,*" he says with a sleepy smile on his face.

It seems that things worked out at least for the moment, and I was neither kicked out nor arrested. So now assertively I said:

"*Pepe, tua novia Cristina,* sent me to you to buy some *artesania*".

"*Oh, Cristina, mi amor,*" he moaned.

"She told me to tell you she loves you very much".

"Oh, Cristina is such a nice girl. *La amo tanto.* We'll soon get married...." he paused for a moment, lost in thought.

Married? I thought. Maybe when you get out of this jail...

"But, if you want to see *artesania, siguro*. I have it in the cell. Wait a moment," and he walked away fumbling with his belt. Meanwhile, the guardian gave up fitting his belt and went back to his room, holding his pants with one hand.

After a minute, Pepe came out with a wooden box. Inside were several statues and a *rongorongo* tablet, bearing the sculpted characters of the still-undeciphered script. There are 'only' 15,000 glyphs with too few comparatives to allow the script to be deciphered, at least for now. I asked him for the prices, and, as Cristina had said, they were lower than those in the market, and I bought a tablet and a wooden *moai* statue. I still could not believe that it had happened. It was like a dream: I was inside a jail, and I bought 'stuff' from one of the inmates, and now I have to sneak out. I thanked and paid Pepe directly in US dollars, turned around, and left the courtyard. I didn't push the bolt of the gate, and I could hear the gate squeaking in the wind as I walked away towards the road. I still felt uneasy about the whole encounter, and when I reached the road and turned my head, I was startled to see both Pepe and his fellow inmate leaving the jail, waving at me as warmly as if we had known each other for a lifetime.

"Oh, my God, what did I do? I helped the inmates escape. I left the gate open, and they took advantage of the guard who was sound asleep and escaped through the jail's front gate. I was part of this escape. I became an accomplice by leaving the gate open."

These thoughts followed me until I arrived at the residence. I hurriedly packed, praying I could get on the plane before the guardian discovered that I had freed the inmates. Maybe they were killers or rapists, and now they were on the loose, attacking somebody else. My paradise was shattered, morphed in those moments into the worst hell with all sorts of scenarios running through my mind. The taxi came to take me to the airport and my freedom. If only I could get through the police and customs and make it onto the plane. I'll figure out what to do once I arrive in Santiago, five hours from now.

The cabbie was relaxed, like everybody on this island, a far cry from my anxiety. I could not stop thinking about what happened and asked him:

"You know, I meant to ask you. I walked on the road today and I saw the jail. Who are the ones jailed there? Are they dangerous?"

He looked at me with a puzzled expression like …I was from New York. Ehh, actually, I was from New York!

And with a big smile, asked back:

"Why do you ask?"

"You know, a girl sent me there to buy some *artesania,* and I met a guy. Pepe…"

"Oh, Pepe," and he smiled. "Yes, he is a very good *artesano* and such a nice guy".

"OK, but how come he is in jail if he is such a nice guy? Did he rob anybody?" I was afraid to ask if anybody was hurt or killed in the heist.

On his face, I could read bafflement followed by a way bigger smile:

"*No, amigo*," he continued to smile. "I don't know what he did, but probably he drank too much one evening, and he made some fuss in a bar."

Encouraged by his relaxed response, I continued my interrogation:

"Yeah, but I am concerned that I left the gate open, and I saw them leaving the jail. Pepe and his cellmate. I was worried that I helped them escape."

Now the driver laughed from the depths of his heart.

"*Oh, no, no, no.* You don't get it," and more laughing.

"They do not stay in jail overnight. They go home. They have families, and it is pointless to stay there overnight. They went home and would return tomorrow morning for several hours. It's not like in those movies..."

I was relieved. I was off the hook, but the most important thing was that my paradise was not lost. The plane was waiting on the tarmac, and I walked towards it with no sign of police, security, immigration, or customs agents around, just showing my ticket at the door.

CHAPTER 21

The Mystery of a Journey

I'VE ALWAYS WONDERED WHAT WE MISS NOW THAT everything seems to be at our fingertips. I should feel a great sense of joy that everything is just a click away, that I can go anywhere, anytime, just by clicking the mouse button and calling an Uber to take me to the airport. Even visas for certain countries, if required, can be obtained with just a few clicks. On the way to the airport, another click and your place to sleep is also secured. With another click, the car waits for you on arrival to take you to the hotel, or maybe directly to a restaurant you booked with another click. The hotel has a rating, as does the restaurant and the car rental place.. And every place you want to visit has its own rating based on the feedback of previous visitors. When you reach your destination, another click translates your question into the local language, and—perhaps surprisingly—the person you ask pulls out their phone and answers it with a single click. Congratulations! You talked with the first person on the other side of the globe without exchanging a word.

You may sometimes feel there's no point in going anywhere in the world since you can see everything on your phone, straight from your bed. But perhaps it's precisely because everything seems so accessible that few places in the world still preserve that forgotten, secret flavor. And that's not because the times before the Internet were better or because you were there decades ago, which implanted in your mind a remembrance of youth and adventure's perfume.

When the Internet was still a futuristic illusion, travel guides read like novels. You were trying to find in them the most interesting places you wanted to discover in the limited time you had. The few pictures in the guidebook, rare at the time even for a travel guide, were the subject of a whole analysis that may have convinced you whether or not to go to a certain place for a day, or to spend that precious vacation day elsewhere. Graphic options were rare. Maybe just a stray scrapbook in a bookstore, with pictures of the country you were planning to visit or some friends' slides who traveled there, but nothing more. The recommended books offered a glimpse of the local culture, but without adequate pictures, they left you clueless about what to expect. The route you took was, in fact, a series of attempts, trying to mark dots on the map and hoping that along the way you would meet other travelers like yourself, who would reveal new, wondrous places they had discovered along the way. These travelers continued to provide information in the early days of Internet travel groups, which were then accessible only through university networks.

So, off you went on an adventure shrouded in mystery that you desperately tried to unravel by reading the book of the secrets of that world that was then the Lonely Planet. All you carried with you was a plane ticket, the guidebook you never parted with, a few foreign languages if you were lucky enough to know them, and a bag of dollars you exchanged at the borders. You didn't have reservations at hotels whose numbers were small, you ate wherever you could without a Yelp recommendation, you didn't know how you were going from one place to another, crushed by the crowds rushing to buy a train ticket, or on the lookout for an elusive bus to the destination where you wanted to go. All was veiled in enigma, and it was this very air of mystery that lent the journey its special allure. You were discovering something that only a few others, also adventurers you'd met by chance at a party in Brooklyn or on the way, had explored in the distant worlds you'd read about in dusty, forgotten books. But what you had, and no one could take from you, was precisely this riddle for you to solve during your adventure. You immersed yourself in that conundrum and gradually began to unravel it sheet by sheet, like the layers of an onion, carefully peeling away, with no idea what was hidden behind each layer. This was your own mystery you held deep in your heart, and, as in a game, you had to decipher it in the few weeks you had available for your travel.

Unfortunately, it is precisely this traveling enigma that has magically disappeared in the age of new media. Recently, a friend who had traveled extensively around the world told me after returning from Morocco, where she had first been many decades ago:

"Everything is so predictable. Euros, dollars, credit cards, everything works. There's no mystery anymore, you know from the beginning where you're going and what everything will look like because the Internet is full of photos of the places you visit. The local guide even shows you where to go to take the best picture and put it on Instagram. You don't even have to make a linguistic effort, because everyone speaks English and they all come and tell you about all kinds of movies and series they watch on Netflix, the same as you watched."

If you've been to a place once, what you find when you revisit it a decade later makes you think you've landed in a completely different place and recognize none of the charms you once discovered. Bangkok, where a slice of soft, transparent bread was the delicacy of the day between endless bowls of rice, has become the world's largest bread producer. The city where it was once impossible to get a cup of coffee is now dotted with Starbucks, offering the same menu as in New York or London. The travel agencies where you used to throw your backpack to grab a bite until you got your Burma or Cambodia visa now have their interiors crammed with Samsonite and Delsey suitcases that have replaced the road-weary backpacks.

It's hard to convey to new travelers the thrill of planning a journey along the hippie trail of yesteryear, which began in Istanbul and ended in India—a route now largely closed due to wars and militant groups. Or what you would have had to do to cross into Burma, locked in its barbaric dictatorship, and then cross into Laos without a visa. Or how to cross borders in Central America without being kidnapped on roads, lurking with guerrillas and insurgents attacking you in broad daylight. Now it's all on the Internet, where you can find all the details. But you don't need them anymore, since you can now fly instead of crossing borders by bus or on foot. In the meantime, you sit in an elegant cafe sipping a latte that tastes the same in

Bangkok, Los Angeles, Calcutta, or anywhere in Europe and wait to stroll around the place where you've just landed, which erases all traces of unpredictability. No, I certainly don't regret the explosion of information on the Internet, which serves everything on a platter for even the least curious tourist, leaving no room for unpredictability. But the saddest thing seems to be that those to whom we yarn stories about this ghostly mystery of travel and its elusive, long-gone unpredictability cannot even imagine that such a world existed and will never understand its meaning or its charm. Time marches on, and with it the cavalcade of information, but for those who know how to look, there are still places, much fewer and well hidden, that retain this forgotten mystery. It only depends on whether there are still any explorers left to search for them, ready to leave their comfort zone.

www.ingramcontent.com/pod-product-compliance
Lightning Source LLC
LaVergne TN
LVHW090519110826
845146LV00003B/910

* 9 7 9 8 9 9 4 8 5 9 4 1 4 *